metaLABprojects

The *metaLABprojects* series provides a platform for emerging currents of experimental scholarship, documenting key moments in the history of networked culture, and promoting critical thinking about the future of institutions of learning. The volumes' eclectic, improvisatory, idea-driven style advances the proposition that design is not merely ornamental, but a means of inquiry in its own right. Accessibly priced and provocatively designed, the series invites readers to take part in reimagining print-based scholarship for the digital age. www.metalab.harvard.edu

Series Editor
Jeffrey T. Schnapp

Advisory Board
Ian Bogost (Georgia Tech)
Giuliana Bruno (Harvard VES)
Jo Guldi (Brown)
Michael Hayes (Harvard GSD)
Bruno Latour (Sciences Po, Paris)
Bethany Noviskie (U of Virginia)
Andrew Piper (McGill)
Mark C. Taylor (Columbia)

Art Direction
Daniele Ledda
metaLAB and xycomm (Milan)

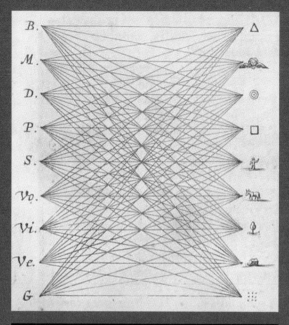

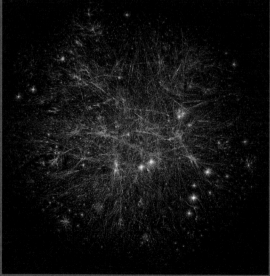

At first these two images
seem remarkably similar. Both appear
to be representations of knowledge
networks made of points and lines.
But one was first published
in 1669 by Athanasius Kircher as
a demonstration of the system of the
medieval mystic Ramon Llull's "great art
of knowing." The other was created
more than three hundred years later.
Generative, diagrammatic, dynamic,
Kircher's image *produces the knowledge
it draws*. By contrast, the recent image
of Web traffic *only displays information*.
It is representation of knowledge,
not a knowledge generator, whose
graphic display conceals the decisions
and processes on which it was based.
Kircher's image was generative and
dynamic by contrast to the fixed
representational image it resembles.

---

(1) Athanasius Kircher, *Ars Magna Sciendi* (1669).
(2) Barrett Lyon, Web Traffic Visualization.

Learning to read these and other visual forms of knowledge production is essential in our contemporary lives. Images are produced and consumed in our current culture in quantities that would have been unthinkable in any previous period in human history.[1] Graphics of all kinds have become the predominant mode of constructing and presenting information and experience. *Graphesis* is the study of the visual production of knowledge, a topic that has compelling urgency in our current environment. (Figures 3 – 4)

This book offers a brief guide to critical languages of graphical knowledge from diverse fields, and describes ways graphical formats embody semantic value in their organization and structures. I make use of historically grounded insights to create an understanding of interface and visualization, but this is not a "history of" visualization, visual knowledge,

(3) Many Mona Lisas: screen grab of search results for images of Mona Lisa.
(4) Visual Complexity: screen grab of the home page of a site hosting information visualizations.

or the technologies and theories of interface any more than it is a systematic study of new media/data art. Rather than a chronologically organized study of the unfolding of graphic traditions, it is an outline of principles and precepts that structure visual forms of knowledge production and representation in graphic formats. This emphasis justifies the use of examples from vastly different time periods, images linked by their structuring principles rather than their shared place in time or culture. The grids of early cuneiform tablet accounting systems undergird the tables in spread sheets and railroad schedules—even if their historical appearance is separated by several millennia—because they organize content according to the same graphical means.

The screens on our hand-held and mobile devices, in public displays,

(5) An interface so real you ...

and connected to networked flows, not only flood us with images, they structure our relation to knowledge *visually*.[2] (Figure 5)

This ubiquity of graphical formats calls for a new critical understanding of the ways we read and process visual information. Learning to read the meaning-producing argument structures of graphical forms is a challenge, since the traditions of art history focus on iconography among other elements, those of traditional graphic design on layout, legibility, and style, and those of diagram and graph theory on principles of logic. We need to develop a domain of expertise focused on visual epistemology, knowledge production in graphical form in fields that have rarely relied on visual communication.

The majority of information graphics, for instance, are shaped by the

(6) Virtual globes prismmap uses the illusion of three-dimensional volume with mixed results.

disciplines from which they have sprung: statistics, empirical sciences, and business. Can these graphic languages serve humanistic fields where interpretation, ambiguity, inference, and qualitative judgment take priority over quantitative statements and presentations of "facts"?

To begin, a brief gloss on a number of terms crucial to our discussion will establish a common vocabulary: **information graphics, graphical user interface, visual epistemology,** and the phrase "**languages of form**" or its variants, "visual language," "graphic language," and so on.

Information graphics are visualizations based on abstractions of statistical data. *All information visualizations are metrics expressed as graphics.* Visualizations are always interpretations—data does not have an inherent visual form that merely gives rise to a graphic expression. (Figure 6)

(7) Lisa Synder, The World's Columbian Exposition of 1893. Screen grab of visual simulation model of the Exposition showing source materials embedded in the project.

Graphical user interface is the dominant feature of screens in all shapes and sizes. *No single innovation has transformed communication as radically in the last half century as the GUI.* In a very real, practical sense we carry on most of our personal and professional business through interfaces. Knowing how interface structures our relation to knowledge and behavior is essential. (Figure 7)

Visual epistemology refers to ways of knowing that are presented and processed visually, though in this book I only pay attention to representations, not to cognition. Visual expressions of knowledge are integral to many disciplines in the natural sciences, but language-oriented humanities traditions have only barely engaged with visual forms of knowledge. Creating new forms of argument in graphical forms will be a challenge. (Figures 8 – 9)

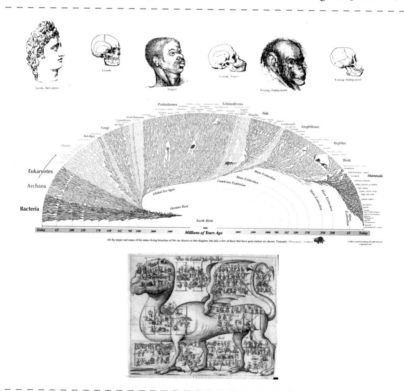

(8) Josiah Clark Nott and George Robert Gliddon, *Indigenous races of the earth* (1857).
(9) Leonard Eisenberg, visualization of evolution: *Great Tree of Life* (2008).
(10) Johannes Buno, *Universae historiae cum sacrae tum profanae idea* (1672): a fanciful depiction of historical eras with section showing the fourth millennium before the birth of Christ.

The phrase **"language of form"** suggests a systematic approach to graphic expression as a *means* as well as an *object* of study. The long history of codifying knowledge in visual forms contains a rich inventory of examples on which to construct a fundamental understanding of graphics as systematic expressions of knowledge. (Figure 10)

With these concepts in play, our task is three-fold. First, to study information graphics and begin to understand how they operate; to de-naturalize the increasingly familiar interface that has become so habitual in daily use; and finally, to consider how to serve a humanistic agenda by thinking about ways to visualize interpretation. (Figures 11 – 12 – 13 – 14)

The task of making knowledge visible does not depend on an assumption that images represent things in the world. Graphics make and

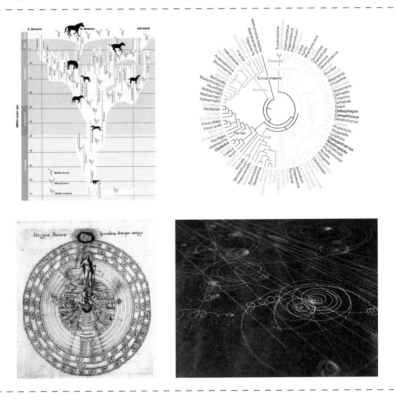

(11) Bruce MacFadden, "Patterns of Phylogeny and Rates of Evolution in Fossil Horses: Hipparions from the Miocene and Pliocene of North America," *Paleobiology* 11.3 (Summer 1985): 245-57.
(12) Algorithmically generated tree of phylogeny in radial form.
(13) Robert Fludd, *Utriusque Cosmi, Maioris scilicet et Minoris, metaphysica, physica, atque technica Historia* (1617).
(14) Cloud chamber with tracks of particles.

construct knowledge in a direct and primary way. *Most information visualizations are acts of interpretation masquerading as presentation.* In other words, they are images that act as if they are just showing us *what is*, but in actuality, they are *arguments made in graphical form.* (Figures 15 - 16)

But paradoxically, the primary effect of visual forms of knowledge production in any medium—the codex book, digital interface, information visualizations, virtual renderings, or screen displays—is to mask the very fact of their visuality, to render invisible the very means through which they function as argument. The purpose of this book is to call these visual forms of knowledge production to our attention and provide a descriptive critical language for their analysis. The particular emphasis is on *humanistic* forms of knowledge production and critical study of visuality

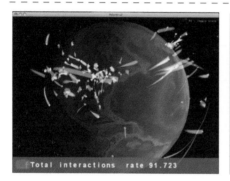
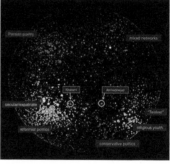

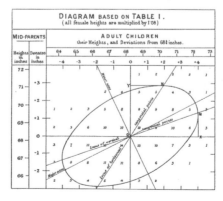

(15) Facebook activity visualization.
(16) Francis Galton, axes to communicate statistical variables in height of mother and daughter plants (1875); from Karl Pearson, *The Life, Letters, and Labours of Francis Galton* (Cambridge: University Press, 1914-1930).

from a humanistic perspective. The design solutions used in many projects—buying books online or checking for directions in a digital map—are quite adequate for the purpose they serve. But visual forms of knowledge production have always suffered from suspicion by contrast to the unambiguous capacities of numerical and textual representation. Now is the moment to lift that ban of suspicion and engage the full potential of visuality to produce and encode knowledge as interpretation. (Figure 17)

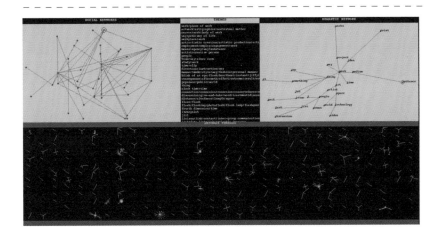

(17) Warren Sack, Conversation Map (2003).

For Jane Drucker,
the best and most dedicated reader of my work

Johanna Drucker

++++++++++++++

Graphesis
Visual Forms
of Knowledge
Production

metaLABprojects

- - - - - - - - - - - -

Harvard University Press

Cambridge, Massachusetts, and London, England

2014

Library of Congress Cataloging-in-Publication Data

Drucker, Johanna, 1952-
  Graphesis : visual forms of knowledge production / Johanna Drucker.
    pages cm. — (MetaLABprojects)
  Includes bibliographical references.
  ISBN 978-0-674-72493-8 (alk. paper)
    1. Visual communication. 2. Graphic arts. 3. Information visualization. 4. Visual analytics. I. Title.
  P93.5.D78 2014
  302.23--dc23

                          2013050669

Graphic Design:
xycomm (Milan)
Gennaro Cestrone
Stefano Cremisini
Edda Bracchi

Table of Contents

Image,
Interpretation,
and Interface

Even though our relation to experience
is often (and increasingly) mediated
by visual formats and images, the bias
against visual forms of knowledge production is longstanding in our culture.[3]
Logocentric and numero-centric attitudes prevail. Vision has served knowledge in many ways across the sciences,
arts, and humanities in theoretical and

applied domains. Attention to style, iconography, and other formal properties is well developed in the fine arts, where concerns with connoisseurship and the social function of images drive the field. We also know that pictorial images reveal much about the history of visual culture and knowledge and that familiar art historical theories and methods are used for their analysis. Despite its sophisticated knowledge of visual production, art history has not focused on visual epistemology as a primary concern. For a brief period in the formative stages of modernism, particularly in the early decades of the twentieth century, concerns with formal systems of visual expression brought major artists such as Wassily Kandinsky and Walter Crane into discussion of graphical knowledge production.

The field of visual epistemology draws on an alternative history of images produced primarily to serve as expressions of knowledge. For the study of graphesis, attention to fine art images will be largely left aside in favor of attending to the vast array of visual work produced for the purposes of interpretation or analysis in other fields. For different reasons, but by the same logic, graphic design works will also be left out of this discussion, except for the subset that overlap with information visualization, such as the elaborate work of Otto Neurath or studies by Anton Stankowski. Since we inhabit a world permeated by digital technology, we will address the urgency of finding critical languages for the graphics that predominate in the networked environment: information graphics, interface, and other schematic formats, specifically in relation to humanistic problems of interpretation. To do this we can draw on the rich history of graphical forms of knowledge production that are the legacy of manuscript and print artifacts as well as digital media works in the arts and applied realms.

The language of graphics

Many attempts have been made to create an explicit, stable, universal, and rule-bound language of graphics. Such a language actually has two aspects: a highly formal set of visual elements with rules for their use and a verbal description of this system and the ways it works.

The most complete graphic language systems appear in the twentieth century, as adjuncts to design curricula and professional training. They played a crucial part in the "research" agendas that were part of visual art's claim to cultural authority in the modern era. Work at the Bauhaus, as well as in the technical academies and design schools founded in the 1920s and 1930s, such as Vkhutemas in Moscow, fostered a brief but generative dialogue between visual practices of design and those of fine art. Graphic design became a distinct profession in this period, while the fine arts absorbed the formal lessons of modern abstraction into aesthetic concerns. Visual epistemology may have been integral to engineering, architecture, industrial design, textiles, cartography, scientific illustration, and statistical analysis, but it failed to become a separate field among academic disciplines. Information visualization, graphics in the service of quantitative methods, remained a subset of business, economics, statistics, and other fields where the use of charts, graphs, and diagrams proliferated. Fine artists had only intermittent interest in these matters until the recent wave of data art and visualization work became a conspicuous trend in digital practices.[4]

Though ignored by fine arts for most of its history, the systematic production of graphic knowledge has a very long tradition. For instance, we could track into the records of antiquity and examine treatises on geometry that have left their trace in the scant but precious remains of written documents from Egypt and the ancient Near East. We can argue that visual knowledge can be considered codified as soon as the graphic forms of triangles, squares, circles, and arcs are described in drawings and texts.[5] These treatises are not drawing or design manuals, but they are graphical expressions of mathematical, logical, knowledge in a systematic visual and verbal form. By contrast to such mathematical treatises, the works that comprise the "language" of graphic communication centuries later are more rhetorical than logical, and their features can be described in terms of visual principles that relate to sight, perception, cognition, cultural conventions, and norms. All of these investigations of visual forms as a systematic expression of knowledge contribute to the search for a "language" of graphics.

The links between knowledge and visuality not only have historic roots, they have historical and cultural dimensions. Our ideas about images and even vision are different from those common in earlier epistemic moments. We no longer believe in the Roman Lucretius's imaginative idea that vision is produced when films float from the surface of objects into our eyes—any more than we believe a picture goes from our eye to our head like a letter being delivered by a postman or a fax being transferred across a wire.[6] The representational approach to vision is passé. We now know that the affordances of our senses and the capacities of cognition together construct the impression of a visual world. The world we see is a world made by our cognitive ability. Indigenous peoples map their territory in vastly different conventions than western cultures, and with a different orientation to the globe itself. The point? Images have a history, but so do concepts of vision and these are embedded in the attitudes of their times and cultures as assumptions guiding the production and use of images for scientific or humanistic knowledge.

The theoretical, methodological foundation for graphesis as the visual approach to knowledge production has to be cobbled together from a variety of contributing intellectual traditions, each with its own disciplinary roots. These approaches to the systematic understanding of visual epistemology will form the core of my approach:

- Knowledge and/as vision: the ways visual ordering and classification serve intellectual work, particularly with respect to issues of interpretation;
- Languages of form: the formal systems in which visual forms have been classified and characterized;
- Dynamics of form/universal principles of design: the extension of the "languages" metaphor to universal and dynamic systems;
- Gestalt principles and tendencies: the principles of perception that locate visual knowledge in psychology and human experience;
- Basic variables: the contributions of the semiotics of graphics;
- Understanding graphics and editing: techniques of framing and reading;
- Processing images: basic issues in computational vision; and finally,
- Typology of graphic forms presents ways of classifying graphic images in current use for humanistic projects.

These topics do not offer a history of information visualizations per se, but they do provide a historical and critical foundation for understanding formal graphic languages in information visualizations and graphical user interface as adopted to the humanistic domains from a vast array of sources.

Knowledge and/as vision

Vision was given highest priority in the hierarchy of senses among the Ancients, and then, from the late Middle Ages through the Enlightenment, human vision was augmented through the use of technical instruments. Perhaps these factors intensified the belief that the workings of the natural world might be made apparent to and through the eye, and that careful observation was the key to unlocking the workings of the universe.[7] What could be seen could be known, and knowledge and sight had a reliable connection even if visual means of representing that knowledge were taken for granted rather than studied in their own right. Observation and recording were used since ancient times to diagram the movements of the heavenly bodies, to make an inventory of botanical specimens in manuscript production before the age of print, or to chart a course navigating partially known or unknown territories. Different technologies and media play their role in knowledge production as surely as do changes in optical instruments and observational techniques. Study of the specificity of graphic media has its own critical tradition.

For example, the art historian William Ivins stressed the full impact of copperplate engravings, and their ability to produce "exactly repeatable statements," on the fields of natural history as well as fine art in the fifteenth and sixteenth centuries. Later, lithographic and photographic capacities added naturalistic accuracy to visual images in widespread circulation.[8] Mechanistic reproduction expanded and various mass media used new techniques for the creation of visual culture.[9] Expectations about images changed and even the concept of what constitutes a likeness alters over time. We come to believe that photographs are an unmediated image, what Roland Barthes called an "image without a code," and continue this belief as digital methods of scanning, altering, and creating have developed.[10] But of course, all images are encoded by their technologies of production and embody the qualities of the media in which they exist. These qualities are part of an image's information. Just think how quickly image quality in digital output or even screen resolution becomes identified with a particular moment in history. Woodblocks, daguerrotypes, silver nitrate black and white film, Technicolor, or early digital animation signify by their production features as well as their contents. The emerging field of media archaeology puts attention to the specificity of production means at the center of its methods, reading the matter of media as the foundation on which they configure meaning.[11]

When the late sixteenth century Dutch engraver, Johannes Stradanus, set out to create a suite of prints showing the inventions that had produced modern life, *Nova Reperta*,

he subscribed to the belief that every aspect of human knowledge could be communicated visually. But times change, and paradigms shift. We are keenly aware that the breadth and depth of contemporary knowledge exceeds the capacity of visual presentation. We no longer believe that everything that can be known can be seen

Johannes Stradanus, illustration of copperplate production, from his *Nova Reperta* (1638).

any more than we believe in the "truth" of visual images. Though we often use visual means to make images of invisible things, much of contemporary life simply can't be shown. The workings of power, the force of ideology, the transmission of values, and other abstract ideas have no specific visual form, even if they work through a material social world.

Speed, scale, complexity, and the infrastructure in place and at work in systems of communications, production, distribution, much scientific discovery, and humanistic thought simply cannot be made apparent in visual images. But an endless stream of visualizations continues to turn complex phenomena into images, reifying abstractions, turning them into objects to be seen.

At the same time, in spite of its widespread use, visual representation remains suspect as a form of knowledge. The mathematician René Thom once stated unequivocally that knowledge could only be communicated using one of two modes of expression: mathematical notation and written language.[12] He deliberately excluded graphical means as unreliable. Visual codes are notoriously unstable, too imprecise to communicate knowledge with certainty. And humanistic visual knowledge was bracketed out of his account with particularly good reason: its methods threaten the very foundations of epistemological stability and mathematical certainty that align with empirical tenets.

Thom had good reason to be suspicious of humanistic knowledge, with its emphasis on interpretative rather than quantitative methods. And he was also correct in his implied assessment that visual images have no single identifiable code, and thus did not meet his standards for scientific notation. Language can be rendered in characters, these can be

Philipp Steinweber and Andreas Koller, convergent and divergent designations of god in Buddhist, Hindu, Islamic, and Christian texts.

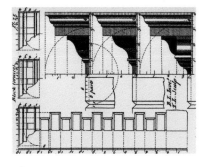

communicated to the computer through keystrokes that link to binary codes in an explicit system. Textual meaning may be ambiguous, but the remediation of alphabetic code into digital form is not. Likewise, numbers represent quantities in an unambiguous way that is stable and repeatable. But the marks and signs that make up an image are neither semantically consistent—that is, they don't represent meaning or value in a dependable way—nor are they graphically consistent, unless they are produced with mechanical means. Even at a higher level of organization, above the basic units, signs, or elements of the system, visual images are not constructed by a given set of rules. Unlike language, which has a grammar, or mathematics, which operates on explicit protocols, visual images are not governed by principles in which a finite set of components is combined in accord with stable, fixed, and finite rules.

But Thom overlooked the ways graphical representation has encoded and communicated knowledge for centuries. Systematic uses of visual images have created standards and consensus across a wide variety of disciplines that depend on visual observation and analysis.[13] Architecture provides a particularly useful example of this since analogies with language as a formal system were central to description and analysis of building styles from late antiquity. The classic text of Vitruvius, composed late in the first century, contained a typology of architectural forms that became the basis of western Renaissance writings on the topic.[14] Sebastiano Ser-

Batty and Thomas Langley, *The Builder's Jewel, or the Youth's Instructor, and the Workman's Remembrancer,* plate 75 (1741).

lio's *Regole generali d'architettura*, first published in 1537, for example, presented Vitruvius's classical orders as a set of rules governing visual organization.[15] Like Andrea Palladio's 1570 *I quattro libri dell'architettura*, Serlio's text codified Vitruvian principles and became the reference for all later description of the elements of classical architectural design.[16] Not only did these works present a set of terms and references, but, more significantly for our discussion, they put firmly in place the concept that a visual system might be structured like a language. Style, motif, texture, color, and materials all aligned with semantic elements while relations, composition, sequence, narrative were considered parts of a syntactic function. This concept could, and would, be adopted in many other fields. Its roots in classical form appealed to the Renaissance sensibility, its apparent rational ordering principles to Enlightenment thought, and the articulation of universal formal principles to modernists trying to find a scientific basis for visual work.

Architectural styles could be described as a language by using language, but they also relied on the use of graphic techniques that supported visual comparison and inscribed features of style, proportion, and decoration. These were imitated over and over, and became so conventional that the initial innovation in graphic presentation came to be taken for granted. This is true in other fields as well where visual presentation is essential for the purpose of communication or analysis. Herbalists, astronomers, navigators, and medical practitioners depended on visual information even if a theory of visual epistemology was not made explicit until much later. A handful of major precedents ap-

Ephraim Chambers, the classical orders, *Cyclopaedia, or Universal Dictionary* (1728).

pear earlier, but the gap between the use of visual images to communicate knowledge and the development of the concept of a "language of graphics" was only closed in the twentieth century—when formalized rules of visual communication were articulated in very deliberate terms.

Like architecture, the study of physiognomy depended on visual forms, but it is an entirely interpretative system. Giambattista Della Porta's analysis of character, *De Humana physiognomonia*, published in 1586, connects visual experience to assessment.[17] Through examination and representation of facial features, skull proportions, expressions, and postures, the work classifies through depiction. Porta created a systematic analysis that depended on making links between visual features and value judgments about character. Visual images and physiognomy remained bound to each for centuries, even across changes of media. Johann Kaspar Lavater's later work on physiognomy, published between 1775–1778, got much of its long-standing rhetorical force from its engraved images while the famous French forensic investigator, Alphonse Bertillon, used photographs of hundreds of criminals in order to affirm his convictions about degenerate character types and their ability to be detected visually.[18] Physiognomy exemplifies

Darwin's finches, a study in beak adaptations, *Voyage of the Beagle* (1845).

Rodolphe Toepffer's graphic inventory of profiles, *Essay zur Physiognomie* (1845).

a specific method of producing interpretative knowledge and social consensus in and through graphic representations. Caricaturists made good use of these methods, playing on the ways graphic codes established categories and provoked specific associations in viewers. In both cases, architecture and physiognomy, the information embodied in physical form becomes codified through graphic representation.

Graphic methods are crucial to scientific work, either for recording observation, expressing results, testing hypotheses, or formulating projects within the terms of epistemological debate or at its edges. Etienne Marey's 1878 *La Méthode graphique* was premised on the recognition that certain scientific investigations required graphic means for the precision they offered in circumstances where language failed.[19] His photographic studies of motion introduced techniques of analysis that were specifically visual, breaking the continuum of movement into discrete images for study. But the analysis of graphics as a system, one that could be governed by predictable rules, explicitly articulated, arose within the visual arts. Specifically, these systems of rules arose in the arena of applied drawing useful for industry and engineering. In these realms drawing was more linked to surface organization of elements that provided plans and patterns for production than to the creation of pictorial illusion.

Drawing manuals and treatises on painting created by fine artists were too heavily linked to the study of classical statues, systems of proportion and harmony, and perspectival rendering of space and atmospheric effects, to develop analysis of purely formal elements of graphic production and composition.[20] They focused on pictorial principles, approaches to shade, rendering, or inspiration—as in Leonardo's famous suggestion to use a smudge or stain or blot of dirt as a hallucinatory point of departure for drawing.[21] The very idea of graphic-ness, attention to the surface of a visual plane on which compositional elements interacted—not merely as representations of other things, but as elements in themselves—required a conceptual leap. Just as we associate

D'Arcy Thompson, models of formal mutation from *On Growth and Form* (1917).

the self-referential attention to the picture plane with a phase of visual modernism, so we can note that, for all the evidence that cave painters, Egyptian muralists, Native American weavers, medieval illuminators, or Islamic tile-makers understood how to create dynamic compositions using the elements of graphic design on a plane surface, the systematic articulation of a graphic method only started to appear in the nineteenth century. The full intellectual import of this oversight can be grasped if we were to imagine, by analogy, that no explicit grammars had been written until the same period. The rules that govern language structures, combination, and use have been in existence for thousands of years, as have the rules of mathematics and music. This makes the relatively recent, and still partial, articulation of principles of graphics that much more astounding.

Languages of form

In 1856, a milestone work brought the metaphor of visual language into focus. *The Grammar of Ornament*, produced by Owen Jones, was a massive, monumental sourcebook, a comprehensive encyclopedia of decorative motifs

Owen Jones,
*The Grammar
of Ornament*
(1856).

taken from every cultural and historical period known to Victorian Britain.[22] It embodies the imperial impulse of its time and place by the sheer comprehensive exhaustion of range and reach. Persian, Indian, Chinese, African, Indonesian, Polynesian, and other indigenous and exotic designs are among the scores of styles presented alongside those from antique, medieval, and Renaissance sources in Western culture. As graphic art, the stunning chromolithographed pages exhibit a rational and systematic approach to the presentation of ornament in both semantic and syntactic modes. The semantic modules are iconographic elements, figures, isolated units of organic or geometric design. The syntactic elements are strips or fields of motifs exhibiting continuous, interwoven, repeated units and patterns combined in integrated compositions as well as the overarching compositional structure of each page in relation to the whole system of the book. For Jones, grammar is not just a concept to be invoked or waved at, but a structuring principle to be engaged in the production of his own project even if he did not say these things explicitly. Jones did not divide his "grammar" into semantic and syntactic operations, but he offered examples that can be described in these terms.

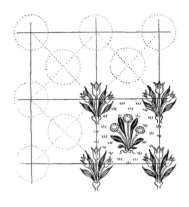

Jones produced the most ambitious pattern book in the history of Western art, and he made skilled use of graphical means and principles, but his purpose was not to spell out the rules of graphic language. Other individuals would do this, equally concerned with the relations between industrial production (Jones was providing the textile, ceramic, and decorative paper manufacturers with a goldmine of inspiration) and visual techniques. New training demands arose as industrial, applied arts were put in the service of the production of artifacts, wall-coverings, books, posters, textiles, and other mass produced objects. This created a need for systematic education in creation of pattern and form, shape and design, not pictorial illusion. In such a cultural context, graphic arts had a role to play at a different scale than in the past eras

Walter Crane, *Line and Form* (1900).

David Pierre
Humbert
de Superville,
synoptic table
from *Signes
Inconditionnels
de l'art* (1827).

of artisans and illuminators. Objects of manufacture had to be patterned from flat sheets of wood, metal, tin, and cloth, just as surely as decorative motifs had to be created for automated print production. Thinking in graphic terms served production exigencies tailored to the tolerances of machines, not hands, knowledge that had to be systematized in order to be passed on effectively. The "language of graphics" became a language for and of industry, even as analysis of abstract visual form became one of the distinctive features of late nineteenth century aesthetics and its legacy to twentieth century modernism. The rhetoric of supposedly universal formal principles is historically coincident with the need for an abstract graphical approach to design for industrial production.

But interest in affect and effect, emotional force of communication and predictable impacts, play a part in the investigation of graphic forms as well. Just as these systematizations of visual languages emerged, another intriguing harbinger appeared: Humbert de Superville.[23] His analysis of configurations of line and compositional features as expressions of affective and emotional conditions was presented as a system in his 1827 study of "absolute" qualities of visual art. Superville's *Essay on Non-conditional Signs in Art* isolated features of graphical elements, such as diagonal lines, to argue that their effect was universal. While his work borrows from physiognomic analysis, and from the typologies of Renaissance drawing, the attention to dynamic principles of lines and configurations has kernels of the rigorous formalism that became so prevalent in design manuals a century later. Superville was focused on graphic values he believed were universal, an attitude that would infuse the twentieth century modern arts with theoretical premises. Combined with his primitive attempt at systematicity, this provided a crucial early contribution to methods of graphical knowledge.

30

In France, instruction in drawing for industrial purposes became systematized in the late nineteenth century following a proposal put forth by Eugène Guillaume, sculptor and educator, who saw that the old techniques of copying classical statues, studying Renaissance methods of perspective, and/or learning the Beaux Arts approaches to rendering were not going to produce a generalized graphic language suitable to industry.[24] Guillaume understood that it was necessary to cut ties to fine arts in order to produce a practical system based in geometry, not the human body. This put his approach at odds with the history of training in the fine arts. We can think of this as a kind of machine-readable graphic language, long before the advent of digital technology. His emphasis was on knowledge of creating curves that could be stamped or cut by a die, rather than rendered with exquisite precision in charcoal or graphite. Titles invoking a "grammaire" of drawing became conspicuous as foundations for instruction as the nineteenth century came to an end. Design was uncoupled from the task of life drawing, but interestingly, not from the communication of affective experience. Superville's principles of the communicative effect of graphical means found a continuation and echo in Charles Blanc's *La Grammaire des arts plastiques* published in 1870, and the description of affective, emotional, and symbolic features of graphic elements was central to the work of turn of the century theorists, as we shall see in a moment.[25] So even as geometric, linear, abstract forms essential to industrial design became codified in training manuals, theories of the emotional impact of arrangement—the force of diagonals, emotive qualities of color, or other formal features—developed at the same time.

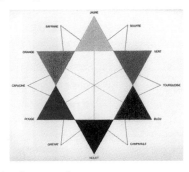

Charles Blanc, illustration from chapter 13, *Grammaire des Arts du dessin* (1867).

Walter Crane, sketches for book layout designs in *Line and Form* (1900).

Right at the end of the nineteenth century, the English illustrator and artist Walter Crane produced two major contributions to graphical analysis: *The Bases of Design* (1902) and *Line and Form* (1900).[26] These two works, though couched in a discursive, descriptive mode, rather than that of a technical manual, are exemplary demonstrations of a methodical approach to a "language" of graphics that proliferated in the twentieth century. Crane had been a student of the widely influential artist and critic, John Ruskin, whose style of careful study, sketching, and observation had formed the basis of his own publications on *The Stones of Venice* (1851-53) and other subjects.[27] Crane's *Line and Form* in 1900 contains a masterful drawing that was a comprehensive inventory of graphic lines and shapes put into a tree-like relation with "parent" forms of square and circle at the base. Crane was a gifted designer as well as a superb illustrator whose approach to composition was dynamic and imaginative, informed by the best work in Western art combined with Asian influences and other diverse sources. Asymmetry, fluidity, movement, and dynamism charged his compositions even when their basic compositional forms had solidity, balance, proportion, and harmony.

[See Window 1, Walter Crane]

What is remarkable about Crane's inventory is not just its attempt at exhaustive presentation, but the structure in which the artist chose to present this knowledge. The tree's root and branch structure echo morphologies from natural and cultural worlds pressed into the service of a graphical one. As a formal system, Crane's image is fraught with contradictions, since the improbability of a square-edged meander arising from a tap root that spawns floral branches above and diagonal repetition nearby renders the organizational trope of the image somewhat irrelevant. But as a conceptual system whose goal is to present the language of graphics in a formalized way, it serves remarkably well as a transition between nineteenth century organicism and twentieth century modern analyses of "graphic languages" or grammars. Crane analyzed the attributes of graphical elements, suggesting that weight, tone, value, pattern, and rhythm each contributed to the identifiable character of an artist's signature style—or that of a period, culture, or ethnic group. Materialist in his methods, Crane was also attached to the analysis of the symbolic character in forms, analyzing the impulse toward conquest in ancient Asiatic art and the generative imagery of the Egyptians. Systematic and replete, Crane's work was meant to train the eye and mind at the same time, providing cultural references and analyses as well as formal means for production.

Dynamics of form/universal principles of design

In the late nineteenth century, the idea that design was a skilled profession whose principles were graphic, not pictorial, and whose "language" was built on an analogy with verbal language began to gain traction. New practices emerged from product and pattern design, analysis of ornament and organization. These needed an explicit articulation of principles that could be taught in a technical training course, not just learned on the shop floor.[28] The rapid escalation of interest in graphic languages for their own sake, and on the development of systematic principles can be marked by shifts from purely technical manuals to those concerned with graphic principles. Late nineteenth century typographic manuals, for instance, contained technical information about composition, typecasting, imposition of pages in complex layouts meant to assist the printer, but no discussion of design principles. These had hardly changed since

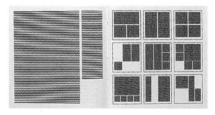

the days of Joseph Moxon's *Mechanick Exercises*, first published in 1694.[29] Almost no systematic or "meta" discussion of graphic design occurs until the field becomes part of curricula in the 1920s, since the very concept of the profession had to evolve from the murky origins of life on the shop floor and at the draftsman's desk. In the first decades of the twentieth century, writings by Jan Tschichold, Frederic Goudy, Bruce Rogers, and Stanley Morison, though very different in taste and orientation, contributed to a growing trend. Attention to composition as an art, not merely a technique, became fully evident for the first time and a full-fledged metalanguage of graphics takes shape.[30] Tschichold stands out among these figures as the person whose statements of principles in *The New Typography* (1928) and *Asymmetric Typography* (originally published in German in 1935) articulated a graphic method, not just a statement of aesthetic belief.[31]

In the early twentieth century, visual artists engaged with modern methods became enthralled with visual abstraction as a formal system. To reiterate, this was a unique and short-lived moment in the history of fine art, a rare engagement with graphical forms rather than problems of formal, iconographic, or conceptual matters. The idea that visual art might have a method that produced reliable and repeatable results gave it an air of authority. Not only were artists interested in the exciting visual possibilities of working with either reductive ("abstracted") forms arranged in a dynamic

Jan Tschichold, *Die Neue Typographie* (1928).

34

manner on a picture plane or "purely formal" ("non-representational") elements, but they were also keen to articulate what they believed were "universal" principles of visual form. Wassily Kandinsky and Paul Klee were among the artists giving voice to these ideas, and they formulated some of the earliest complete theoretical texts.[32] They shared a formative experience at the Bauhaus, and were connected with newly created institutions in the young Soviet state that were working along similar lines. Enthusiasm for the role of the artist in industrial design, synthesis of spiritual principles and formal ones in concepts of universal properties of form (resonance, vibrations, tone as well as compositional effects), and an interest in systematizing approaches to teaching graphic form for applied research and development were all elements of their approach.[33]

This interest in formal methods was part of a broader cultural sensibility in which attempts at formalizing the representation of thought in logic, linguistics, structuralist analyses across cultural domains, and social sciences became prevalent, as evident in the writings of George Boole and Augustus de Morgan taken up by members of the Vienna Circle, such as Gottlob Frege, Rudolf Carnap, and young Ludwig Wittgenstein working at the intersections of logic and language. A direct line connects Boole's 1854 publication *Laws of Thought* to George Spencer-Brown's *Laws of Form*, published a little more than a century later, in 1969. The phrase, "languages of form," adopts these formalisms as the basis of foundation courses in graphic communication. Its roots are in the Bauhaus curriculum developed by these artist-designers keen to produce a systematic approach to visual literacy. Like his earlier 1910 essay, *Concerning the Spiritual in Art*, Kandinsky's 1926 publication, *Point and Line to Plane*, clearly shows the influence of late nineteenth century Symbolist

Fig. 95
Silent lyric
of the four elementary lines—
expression of rigidity.

Fig. 96
Dramatization
of the same elements—
complex pulsating expression.

Use of the eccentric:

Fig. 97
Diagonals centered.
Horizontal-vertical acentric.
Diagonals in the greatest tension.
Balanced tensions of the
horizontal and vertical.

Fig. 98
Everything acentric.
Diagonals strengthened
through their repetition.
Restraint of the dramatic sound
at the point of contact above.

Wassily
Kandinsky,
*From Point and
Line to Plane*
(1926).

synaesthesia, for which music, as much as language, served as the touchstone reference.[34] But it also exhibits the drive toward systematic formalization that was characteristic of the modern sensibility that eschewed historical, literary, and mythological references in favor of an approach to "pure" form. Written from notes originally sketched in 1914, Kandinsky's work is a uniquely creative analysis of visualization. Kandinsky understood vision as a special instance of more universal theories of proportion, harmony, and number. Image and sound were correlates in his system, and the provocative language of his work, combined with its step by step analysis of the properties of points, lines, and planes, remains useful, if idiosyncratic.

Kandinsky isolated a set of primitives of visual composition that are not linked to figurative or literal references. Thus the point is the "proto-element" in his system while the dynamism of lines as forces describes rules that are simultaneously concrete and abstract. Kandinsky's conviction that principles of design crossed the boundaries of media and disciplines kept his vocabulary schematic. Though his terms work to describe visual compositions, they have a logical structure that does not depend on specific visual properties. For instance, in talking of lines, he describes principles of rhythm in terms of repetition, distinguishing quantitative and qualitative aspects of reinforcement that may be achieved in the process. His vocabulary is characteristic of the period in which he was working—references to the fourth dimension show up in words like waves and potentialities. These appear with equal fluency among other figures of dynamism. For instance, he says that the final "Goal of Theory" is to make "pulsation perceptible" and determine "wherein the living conforms to law."[35] This is a striking approach to the dynamic laws of graphic formalism.

Closely related, Paul Klee's *The Thinking Eye*, excerpts from his notebooks in the 1920s, and Laszlo Moholy-Nagy's *The New Vision* (1930) retained conspicuous traces of their artistic origins even as they straddled the traditional divide between fine arts and graphic design.[36] Modernism's codification of visual principles had begun in earnest, and at the same time, the profession of graphic design was taking shape in the context of new communications strategies, advertisement, branding campaigns, and mass market publications. Whether serving public information campaigns or private interests in the business sector, the principles of graphic communication came into sharp focus.[37] Major figures who had been part of the Bauhaus and its peer institutions dispersed to Switzerland, Italy, Britain, the United States, and elsewhere to escape Nazi persecution, spreading the principles of modern design at mid-century.[38] In the period following the end of the Second World War, key institutional players were situated in Geneva, Chicago, New York, Milan, London, and other cities, helping institutionalize an international style of highly self-conscious formal abstraction. This intellectual diaspora had the result of seeding curricula in major institutions around the world. For instance, Moholy-Nagy, whose *Vision in Motion*, published in 1946, outlined the foundation program at the Bauhaus and its extension to the Institute of Design in Chicago where Moholy-Nagy went to work

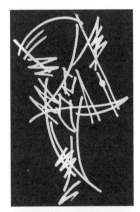

Laszlo Moholy-Nagy, *Vision in Motion* (1946).

as the director in 1937.[39] The major headings of his "Contents" page make clear the integration of organic, sensual, approaches to design and those that link these to machine aesthetics. The section headings in Part II, "Design for Life," give a sense of the totalizing framework in which Moholy-Nagy is outlining his agenda in keeping with the belief that "Designing is not a Profession but an Attitude." The book identified principles of composition organized in relation to basic tenets of dynamism, stasis, order, movement, and other visual fundamentals in a manner that was becoming commonly accepted, but which had only developed through the intellectual efforts of these major thinkers in graphic design.

These texts of early twentieth century designers-turned-teachers or practitioner-theorists became the basis on which the teaching of graphic design was shaped. They were distilled into a set of principles that can be used to create effective communication in visual form. Georgy Kepes's *Language of Vision* (first published in 1944) is far more pragmatic than Kandinksy's spiritual science.[40] "Plastic organization" and "Visual representation," the titles of the two major divisions of his book, are rooted in application to concrete image-making. Other designers, such as the notable Armin Hofmann, wrote texts that outlined "principles of graphic communication" and elaborated tenets of formal visualization as compositional principles (size, scale, movement, order, symmetry, asymmetry, etc.).[41] We take all of this for granted now, but these approaches were innovative in mid-twentieth century design discourse.

By the 1950s, it was commonplace to refer to "graphical language" or "visual communication" as if the comparison were completely natural. In 1973, Donis A. Dondis's classic *Primer of Visual Literacy* contains chapter headings like "The basic elements of visual communication" and "The anatomy of a visual message."[42] The text describes ways that "stress" and "repose" or "levelling" and "sharpening"—among dozens of other characteristics—are attributes of visual systems that can be identified, learned, and made use of in a controlled manner. These properties come to seem self-evident as a result, and the assumption that they inhere in a graphical object goes unquestioned. Dondis's book distills the fundamentals of communication into a clear vocabulary accompanied by schematic images that illustrate basic principles from shape, direction, balance, and motion, to applied principles of predictability/spontaneity or understatement/exaggeration. The lessons are designed for use in the studio, and offer a systematic introduction to graphic composition and visual communication. Neither irony nor self-conscious historical inflection are present, and the text reads with all the confidence of any other technical manual.

Publications on the laws of form, principles governing visual communication, became the standard graphic design manuals in the 1950s and 1960s. Swiss design, with its ordered grids and formal rules, so suited to later wire frame design in onscreen environments, was directly influenced by the Bauhaus through teaching and/or personal connection. Max Bill, Karl Gerstner, and Josef Müller-Brockmann published widely.[43] Gerstner's 1964 *Designing Programmes* announces the ways conceptual work, graphic design, systems theory, and information were beginning to converge.[44] Gerstner outlined a radically new approach to generating form through step-by-step procedures. He saw that designers must be prepared to create programs, not just understand composition and formal properties of graphics. More rigid than Kandinsky or Klee, the Swiss designers popularized the grids and stylistic features of a streamlined, functionalist approach based on a conviction that effects could be controlled, pre-

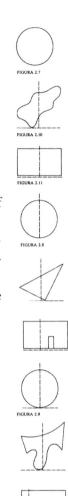

FIGURA 2.7

FIGURA 2.10

FIGURA 2.11

FIGURA 2.8

FIGURA 2.9

Donis A. Dondis, *Primer of Visual Literacy* (1973).

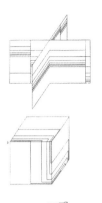

dicted, and produced in accord with rules that could be made explicit. Handbooks for graphic design teaching provided a structured approach to learning lessons of size, scale, texture, orientation, and other compositional principles. Anton Stankowski's daring *Visual Presentation of Invisible Processes* exemplifies graphic design practices that were suited to information display and analysis, even as the world of information visualization and data graphics was exploding in the high-style pages of *Fortune* magazine, *Forbes*, or in the manuals designed to guide the creation of statistical charts and graphs.[45] Like Gerstner, Stankowski pushed graphics into a dialogue with processes that were not inherently visual. If Gerstner used programmatic means to generate graphics, Stankowski used graphic means to express programmatic systems and conditions. The algorithmic sensibility was clearly on the horizon.

Gestalt principles and tendencies

Theoretical study of graphical elements and principles developed somewhat differently in art history than design, at the intersection of cultural anthropology, psychology of perception, and abstract form. Wilhelm Worringer's *Abstraction and Empathy*, published first in 1907, put forth a basic analysis of geometric and organic graphical motifs that is not far from Walter Crane's.[46] Worringer's thesis was that hard-edged, geometric forms emerge in cultures whose relation to the natural world is fraught and difficult, while sinewy curves are found among those in more harmonious circumstances. Worringer's work was highly influential. Carl Jung took some of its principles into his own analysis of symbols and symbolic forms, convinced by the argument for

Karl Gerstner,
*Designing
Programmes*
(1964).

40

specific inherent meaning in icons and images.[47] Worringer's thesis may have been reductive, even essentialist in its claims, but it laid a foundation for consideration of what the elaborate system-maker, Ernst Cassirer, explored across his multi-volume study *Philosophy of Symbolic Form*, published between 1923–29, namely the conviction that forms have value—and that these values have a highly symbolic resonance.[48]

The study of visual perception that resulted in Gestalt principles emerged in studies of psychology in the 1930s.[49] These studies of tendencies of visual form to produce predictable effects had been sparked by the findings of a philosopher, Christian von Ehrenfels. His influential 1890 publication, *On the Qualities of Form*, had reported the observation that a melody's structure, not its specific notes, gave it a distinct formal identity, hence our ability to recognize it across different keys.[50] This principle of "grouping," perhaps better described as a configuration, became the foundation of the work of Gestalt psychologist Max Wertheimer and his collaborators Kurt Koffka and Wolfgang Köhler.[51] Their experimental studies in perception established the existence of certain tendencies in human visual perception. The basic Gestalt principles, proximity, similarity, closure, continuation, common fate, and good form, work in screen environments as well as in print and paper ones.[52] The theorist Rudolf Arnheim studied with the three prominent Gestalt psychologists

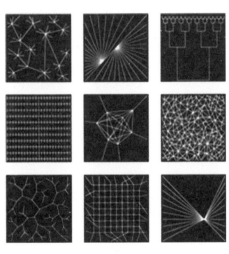

Anton Stankowski, *Visual Presentation of Invisible Processes: How to Illustrate Invisible Processes in Graphic Design* (NY: Hastings House, 1967).

and articulated their principles in his renowned *Art and Visual Perception*, originally published in 1954.[53] Arnheim's treatise is thorough, its application to the visual arts is explicit, and its influence as a text inestimable. The chapter titles show the exhaustive range of his approach: Balance, Shape, Form, Growth, Space, Light, Color, Movement, Dynamics, and Expression. While rooted in perception, the book also became the standard reference for books guiding production. Elaborate as the examples, topics, and issues are, they are in essence reducible, as Arnheim himself states, to "the basic law of visual perception: Any stimulus pattern tends to be seen in such a way that the resulting structure is as simple as the given conditions permit."[54] [See Window 2, Gestalt diagrams]

Basic variables and semiotic approaches

Formalist principles undergird all structuralist and semiotic approaches to the study of form.[55] No text outlining strict structuralist principles in graphic systems (as distinct from the formal approaches of Kandinsky and Klee that emerged in a very different context) was written in the early decades of the twentieth century, though the Russian linguist Roman Jakobson, among others, would later take formal principles derived from the study of poetics into analysis of distinctions between verbal and visual arts.[56] Other early twentieth century semioticians used their linguistic analogies to analyze all manner of cultural practices, including visual ones, but did not create the kind of metalanguage for describing graphics that came from kindred spirits (and sometimes friends and collaborators) working in design in the same period. Semioticians and structuralists struggled to find the basic codes of visual form and only brought these efforts to fruition in the 1960s.

Working through the tenets developed in Russian formalist linguistics in the 1910s and 1920s, Prague School semioticians Juri Lotman, Jan Mukarovsky, and others endeavored to create "systems" for analysis of ritual and performance that could extend Saussurean linguistics to cultural practices.[57] The Prague School's semiotic analyses of fashion and folklore took formal analysis into the realms of culture, including visual culture. These various formalisms divide between those that believe in an inherent quality of graphical expressions themselves (affective qualities of line, shape, movement) and those that are structuralist in their approach to the value of graphic signs in a conventional system (semiotics). Graphical signs trouble the distinction between inherent and conventional meaning production. A diagonal line, for instance, does not represent the angle at which it is drawn, it enacts and embodies its dynamic qualities. But the color red may carry a symbolic value that differs radically across cultures.

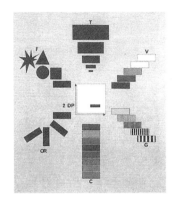

Aesthetician and philosopher Nelson Goodman, whose *Languages of Art* was a late twentieth century classic, proposed systematic tenets for analysis of graphic and pictorial elements.[58] The semiotics of visual forms also found enthusiastic reception from cartographers for whom knowledge and manipulation of basic graphic variables is an essential part of their production. The stabilization of graphical conventions in cartography was driven by needs specific to the profession, but it created insights that can be transferred to other fields. Jacques Bertin's *Semiology of Graphics* (*Sémiologie Graphique*), first published in 1967, embodies a mature ap-

Jacques Bertin (with Marc Barbut et al.), basic graphic variables, *Sémiologie Graphique. Les diagrammes, les réseaux, les cartes* (Paris: Gauthier-Villars, 1967).

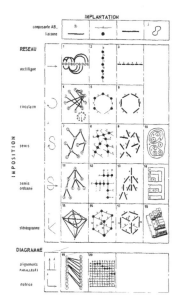

proach to structured analysis of graphical systems for use in design production.[59] Bertin isolated seven variables of static graphics—shape, size, orientation, color, tone, texture, position—and elaborated their considered use for representing cartographic and geographic information. His insights have been adopted by information designers in static and dynamic media, with additional variables (such as rate and direction of movement) specific to the capacities of digital platforms. Assigning statistical variables different roles in a rational way—such as using color to designate intensity, size to show quantity, texture or pattern to another attribute, and so on—gives control over the production of semantic value. In her synthetic work, *Semiotics of Visual Language* (first published in French in 1987), Fernande Saint-Martin presented a more generalized system than Bertin's (which was intimately bound to cartography).[60] The terminology in her table of contents reflects her absorption of the full spectrum of twentieth century writings from a formalist perspective. She begins with "The Basic Elements of Visual Language" and proceeds through such topics as "Syntax of Visual Language" and "The Grammar of Sculpture," and so on. She argued for a concept of the "coloreme" as an equivalent to the "phoneme" in language—the smallest unit of significant meaning production—though, tellingly, the notion did not find widespread acceptance.[61] More pragmatic approaches, less reflexive perhaps and fraught with assumptions, proliferate in books like Robert Horn's *Visual Language: Global Communication for the 21st Century* or the more recent work by Connie Malamed, *Visual Language for*

Jacques Bertin (with Marc Barbut et al.), taxonomy of network diagrams from *Sémiologie Graphique. Les diagrammes, les réseaux, les cartes* (Paris: Gauthier-Villars, 1967).

Designers.[62] Useful as manuals of instruction, as well as analysis of visual principles, such works gloss their structuralist roots and formalist assumptions in favor of providing basic tools for production. The number of titles of text books, design manuals, books meant for trade and school, for artists and designers, that contain some reference to "language" as a part of their systematic approach to form grew substantially in the late twentieth century.[63] Somewhat tempered by issues of ethics, political and social conscience in design, and cultural studies approaches to analysis, the tenets of Gestalt psychology, semiotics, and formal composition remain standard elements of design practice, still applicable to contemporary work.

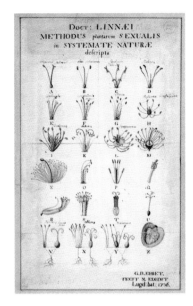

[See Window 3, semiotic principles and graphic variables]

Visual editing/framing and reading

The study of visual elements and systems in formal terms gets augmented when it meets the analysis of narrative sequences and editing practices. Scott McCloud's pioneering work in analyzing comic books and graphic novels provides a useful description of the ways relations across frames can be structured and read.[64] McCloud's approach focuses on the ways graphical frames organize story elements into sense and narrative. The multi-modal and intermedia environments of online viewing require much frame-jumping and shifting, and the overhead on cognition is in large part caused by the way we read the graphical presentation of materials with dif-

Georg Dionysius Ehret's illustration of Linnaeus's sexual system of plant classification (1736); with permission from the Linnean Society of London.

Cross correlations visualized with Pathway Architect text mining software (2011).

ferent requirements for intellectual processing.[65] The transitions that McCloud outlines establish relations between frames (character, place, event, time, story, point of view, detail, and jump) and find their echo in the description of film and video editing. To what extent are the frames in interfaces different from those in comic books and films? Interfaces are spatial and graphic in their use of frames, but these are not necessarily in the service of narrative—rarely, in fact. But film/video, comics, and graphic novels are story-telling forms and the relations across their frames are most frequently used to produce continuity. Random access through motion picture graphics in games, hypertext film, database documentaries, is altering the approach to composition and analysis.

[See Window 4, McCloud and editing principles]

Web environments not only make use of interactive and dynamic graphics, with sliders, time-lines, and animation, but also create spaces in which montage principles and editing techniques used in narrative come into play. The invention of cinema in the early years of the twentieth century introduced time and motion to visual images, as well as the challenge of creating effects across cuts in the celluloid strip. The development of theories of montage bifurcated into

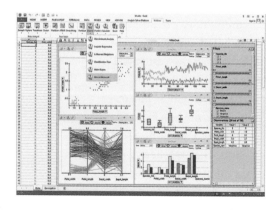

those focused on narrative continuity that dominated Hollywood and other entertainment industries, and those that engaged the exploration of experimental montage, such as the Soviet filmmakers Sergei Eisenstein and Dziga Vertov.[66] Eisenstein's "montage of attractions" methods included metric, rhythmic, tonal, associational, and intellectual (suggestive and symbolic) montage that emphasized both abstract and emotional effects, rather than linear storytelling. Vertov's machine aesthetic was more radical, defamiliarizing, and unfamiliar as a utopian view, and his formalist approaches stressed mechanical motifs. While focused on the literal content of film images, including graphical and formal properties, montage is based on what Roland Barthes termed the "third meaning," or what occurs across images, rather than simply within them.[67]

Editing techniques divide into linear and non-linear approaches, those emphasizing continuity of story through illusions of realism and those that rupture such illusions. Editing techniques have become codified in film schools and video editing classes, whether to optimize realist illusions or to signal avant-garde and innovative departures from standard narrative. Because web environments are dynamic, it is tempting to take the basic language of motion picture editing and create analogies for each kind of shot (close up, establishing, tracking, detail, mid-range, pan, following, and so on), or transition between shots (cheat cut, parallel edit, cut away, dissolve, iris, jump, superimposition, wipe) match across shots (eyeline, action, motion, scene, wipe, shot-reverse-shot, dissolve, jump-cut, etc.), or duration (long shot, overlapping, elliptical, simultaneous). But to reiterate, film editing relies on narrative theory, not just visual principles of perception, and the principles of temporal change, motion, animation, and dynamic graphical means are essential to its production. Web environments force cognitive processing across disparate and often unconnected areas of experience and representation. They frequently require multi-modal processing of varied media. A whole new set of challenges for describing these relational dimensions

arises as a result. As we have seen, between the first decade of the twentieth century and the third, the broad outlines of visual epistemology came into view. From these, semiotic, structuralist, and formal articulations based on the metaphor of a language of graphical means were developed. While theories of vision (these have their own related, independent history) and, even more, those of optics (the science of light, color, and instruments) belong to the history of scientific investigation of the physiology of sight and the phenomena of the visual world, the study of Gestalt principles, design and compositional rules, and visual tendencies are rooted in interpretative activity.[68] The humanistic aspiration to imitate scientific systematization is linked to a modern attempt to develop universal principles, tenets that would obtain in all cultural and historical circumstances. Like structuralism's central principles about systems and values, these assumed that universal principles might transcend their embodiment in instances or expressions. That this is itself an expression of a historical moment, particularly and specifically modern, does not necessarily negate the principles themselves. An eye looking at a line drawing a round shape that nearly closes on itself will tend to see a circle under many circumstances, just not all. One of the questions that arises in contemporary context is whether a machine can be taught the same principles of analysis or production. The task of abstracting principles that can be used for instruction is quite a different matter when a machine, not a human being, has to be trained. In a computational system, every instruction must be explicit, and no experience of the life-world or body can be drawn on in the process.

Harold Cohen, AARON, principles and demonstration (1979).

Computational processing for analysis and production

The idea of using computers to draw, sketch, or present information in graphical form arose with mainframes and plotter pens, but the task of imagining computer vision is even more difficult. The two have a common interest in identifying graphical primitives, whether for production or for analysis. The pioneering work of Harold Cohen serves as one major example.[69] His automated drawing partner, AARON, the platform on which Cohen worked out his systematic approach to visual composition as a set of ways of thinking about figures, grounds, composition, occluded objects, and points of view, serves as one major example of an attempt to build a visually epistemic machine.[70] Most graphical systems for production are based either on pixel values (the tapestry approach) or vector graphics (shapes stored as mathematically described lines, angles, and relations). These lend themselves to computational processing. But Cohen programmed AARON with primitives about the visual experience of the world—trees, faces, landscapes were described as rule sets governing image production.

A very different challenge arose in the design of drawing and painting programs. These had to choose between an analysis of graphic formal primitives (line, fill, texture) and that of production behaviors (stroke, rub, stipple).[71] More recently, specialized programs aimed specifically at the needs of visual and graphic artists have resulted in numerically based approaches, such as the *Design by Numbers* of John Maeda and the Processing language developed by Ben Fry and Casey Reas.[72] As data visualization has advanced, it continues to draw on traditions of charts, graphs, diagrams, trees, and maps to which we will turn our attention in a moment, though of course production operates in computational environments and on graphical displays that are screen-based, rather than print-based, with all the accompanying shifts in aesthetic style.

Graphical primitives also underpin the approach to artificial vision put forth by David Marr in his 1982 book, *Vision: A Computational Investigation into the Human Representation and Processing of Visual Information.*[73] Marr's analysis incorporated somewhat different founding principles than those of the semioticians and cartographers. He was analyzing visual processing, not graphical forms, and so attempted to create a computational model for the ways in which seeing produces differential data for cognitive understanding.

Marr's primitives were very different from those of his predecessors in the graphic arts, and more directly related to models of vision and cognition in neurobiology and psychology. In addition to the three parts of his model—computational, representational, and physical—he described several stages in the realization of visual processing that moved from what he called a primal sketch to a two and ½ dimensional sketch and

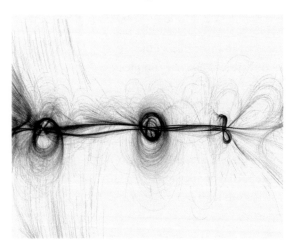

then a final three-dimensional model. The significance of this for our discussion of the languages of graphics is the way he separated edge detection, form recognition, surface treatment, and texture from shape, motion, and depth. Marr broke new ground through such syntheses, and defined visual primitives in terms of the operations through which each property can be processed. He showed that different features of a single image could be isolated and described independently, so that attributes like texture or color were separated from shape or orientation.[74]

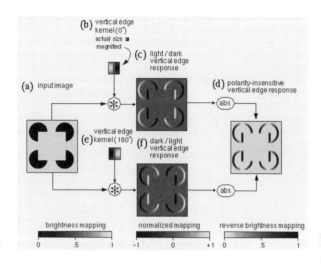

Though many details of Marr's early and posthumous work have been revisited since its publication, its place as a computational theory of visual perception has been questioned and superseded. Artificial vision, whether for analysis or production, still faces daunting challenges. The complexity of visual means of knowledge production is matched by the sophistication of our cognitive processing. Visual knowledge is as dependent on lived, embodied, specific knowledge as any other field of human endeavor, and integrates other sense data as part of cognition. Not only do we process complex representations, but we are imbued with cultural training that allows us to understand them as knowledge, communicated and consensual, in spite of the fact that we have no "language" of graphics or rules governing their use. What we have are conventions, habits of reading and thought, and graphical expressions whose properties translate into semantic value—in part through association with other forms and in part through inherent properties. [See Window 5, David Marr and modelling vision]

Steven Lehar, computational implications of Gestalt theory, figure 4.

From formal languages of graphics to graphic formats

The terms on which formalization occurs are many, as we have seen. In this brief overview, the first examples were of an approach to understanding the affect of graphics, in the work of Superville and others, for whom the emotional, communicative impact was paramount. The early twentieth century modernists, searching for universals, outlined an inventory of effects they believed were absolute, rule-governed, and applicable in all instances (e.g. Crane, Kandinsky). These gave rise to conventions and rules of composition that became the foundation of graphic design curricula and the practice of visual communication (e.g. Dondis, Horn, Moholy-Nagy, Kepes). Contributing to this development in parallel, Gestalt principles were articulated by psychologists interested in perception (Wertheimer, Arnheim). Semioticians took up formal analysis at the intersection of these approaches and created a systematic analysis of elements at the disposal of designers of information graphics, maps, and web environments (Bertin, Saint-Martin). As digital technologies engaged with visual practices, artists and computer scientists engaged the analysis of images to discern the primitives of production and of reception (Cohen, Marr). These formal investigations continue, even as the need for methods suitable to humanistic representations push at the limits of formal means. Obviously, these are not the means required for web interfaces across the board, only within specialized domains where the materials and approaches stress observer-dependent knowledge, interpretative approaches, and depend on our ability to express ambiguity and contradiction. The design of interface and information visualizations (the focus of a coming chapter) has made use of these intellectual traditions while adding its own contributions to the field of knowledge design and graphical form.

This overview of approaches to formal principles of visual communication only skims the surface of a rich history. But the survey demonstrates the existence of carefully thought out foundations on which visual forms of knowledge can be understood. The systematic analysis of "graphical language" remains crucial, its principles are the fundamental basis of graphesis. But they are not its end goal, which is the analysis and imaginative production of visualizations, visualized interpretation, and graphical user interfaces.

Going ahead, we will examine the common forms and conventions used for information visualizations. These often have their origins in antiquity, though many others have come into being more recently to serve modern interests or express computational processes. Our examples draw on long-standing conventions in Western culture and representation. Some of these examples have counterpoints in other cultures—an abacus uses its place-holding apparatus to construct numerical value as surely as columns on balance sheets, tree diagrams have as near a universal presence in ancient cultures as in present ones, and calendars based on a wheel that matches the rotation of the skies with the cycles of the year arise from observations in most indigenous cultures. But other graphical modes are culturally or historically specific. Concepts of fluidity, motion, dynamism that stress ways into and out of a space of graphical composition are more highly privileged in Eastern culture, for instance as opposed to the centralizing symmetries and orderings of the stable picture plane or coordinate mappings of space. In the future, cultural exchanges may result in far more robust and nuanced solutions to our need for interpretative graphics in the humanities.

At the farther edge of speculation, we can approach the

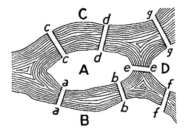

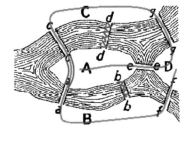

Leonhard Euler's drawings of the Königsberg Bridge problem; from his "Solutio problematis ad geometriam situs pertinentis," *Comment. Acad. Sci. U. Petrop.* 8 (1736): 128-40.

Stephen Wolfram's analysis of the Königsberg Bridge problem.

analysis of graphical forms expressing interpretation through a poetics of relations, with its combination of inflected values and attributes—of hierarchy and juxtaposition, entanglement and embeddedness, of subordination and exchange, and other properties that will be invoked in the discussion of diagrammatic writing in electronic space. Leonhard Euler's struggles with a long-unsolved problem in spatial logic, the Königsberg Bridge problem, established what he called "a geometry of position, not of measure" as a foundational principle.[75] Nineteenth century mathematicians used the word topology, struggling for a language to describe the connectivity of surfaces. Topological vocabulary might well apply to the study of textual structures and paratextual apparatuses and the relations of marginalia, footnotes, margins, columns, spaces, indentations, headers and footers. Theories of editing that engage with continuity and discontinuity are fundamental to reading the rhetorical operations of hyperlinked environments, but we still have a challenge in creating a metalanguage for the ways graphical forms express relations in the extensible space of the screen, and become part of the information of the text through their structuring effects. All graphical schema are built on the single principle of defining classes of entities and of relations. For a humanistic approach, these have to be defined as rhetorical arguments produced as a result of making, a poetics of graphical form, not in the reductive or abstract logics of Boolean algebra. In a humanistic environment, And, Or, and Not, for instance, carry an almost infinite number of qualifying attributes that make each instance distinct. When graphical languages engage with poetics and rhetoric, we will have arrived at a fully humanistic system for visualizing interpretation. For the present, let us turn our attention to the study of graphical forms in information visualizations and interface designs.

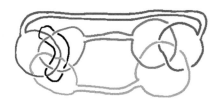

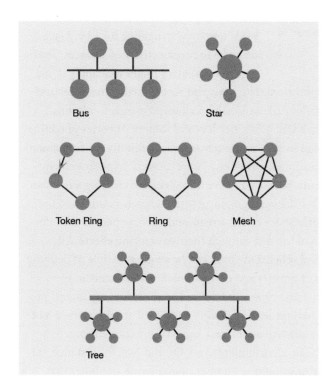

Jacques Lacan, drawing of "The Analytic Situation" (Jan. 14, 1975), quoted from the website of P.L.A.C.E.

Basic topological structures.

Walter Crane's tree

The artist's lively imagination synthesized all the world's decorative motifs into a single tree of pattern systems. The image combines a wealth of specific forms—the Chinese peony, Egyptian lotus, and Arabic leaf among others—with an introduction to basic elements of design. The circle and square form the base—as the *alpha* and *omega* (or "parent forms") —of graphic language from which all other elements can be made.

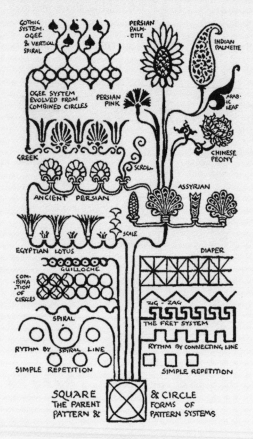

Crane, *Line and Form* (1900).

Gestalt diagrams

The term "gestalt" refers to group-ings and our tendency to see pat-terns wherever possible. Human perception isn't literal. We will close gaps, see motion, make par-tial shapes into whole ones in ways that are surprisingly predictable. Biologists who study perception refer to the "ecology" of vision— ways our visual processes favor needs or tasks essential to our survival. Such ideas counter the old "representational" approach to vision as a "picture in our heads," and replace it with constructivist notions. We don't simply *see* what *is* in a mechanistic way. Instead, *what is seen is what is made.* Instead of talking about pictures and images, we describe visual activity in terms of affordances and processes.

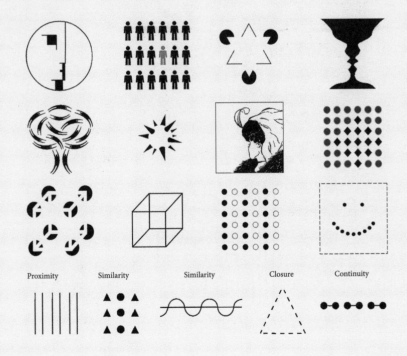

Proximity   Similarity   Similarity   Closure   Continuity

Gestalt diagrams, various sources.

Graphic variables

The cartographer Jacques Bertin identified basic graphic variables for use in mapmaking. His systematic approach has been extremely useful for design in many other fields. The chart below is lacking one of the seven: orientation. This chart neatly summarizes the variables and the best use that can be made of them. Though Bertin's approach, rooted in semiotics (the study of sign systems), was highly rational, it can be used in playful and imaginative ways as well as in highly professional, controlled applications, such as the ones we see in these examples below.

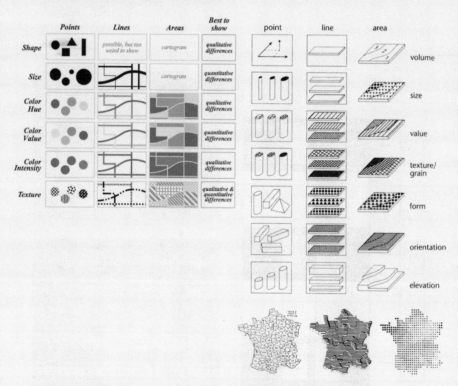

Jacques Bertin, graphic variables,
Semiology of Graphics (1967).

Making connections

Human beings read sequences of images and make sense of them. Comic book artists, film editors, web designers, and graphic novelists all know intuitively how to make connections among images, but Scott McCloud's pioneering work on the graphical structure of comic books offers a systematic description of ways meaning is produced across images. Theorist Roland Barthes used the phrase "the third meaning" to point to the effects of film editing, citing the great Soviet director Sergei Eisenstein as an example. Eisenstein's own work, *Film Form*, is a classic text on editing.

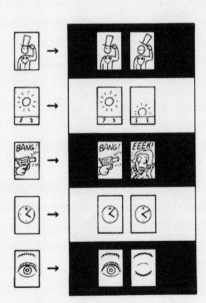

Scott McCloud, editing conventions, *Understanding Comics* (1994).

Sergei Eisenstein, stills from *Battleship Potemkin* (1925).

Modelling vision

The computer scientist David Marr created one of the first models of vision for artificial visual intelligence programming and processing. Trying to teach a computer to process visual experience raised new challenges. Marr had to model the process by which we take in information in visual form. He created a system that could be translated into a computer-driven decision tree by looking at edges, overlaps, surfaces, and other features. His goal was to create the foundation for artificial vision and computational processing of images.

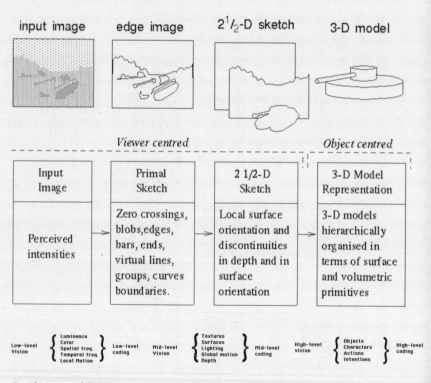

input image   edge image   2¹/₂-D sketch   3-D model

Viewer centred   *Object centred*

Input Image	Primal Sketch	2 1/2-D Sketch	3-D Model Representation
Perceived intensities	Zero crossings, blobs, edges, bars, ends, virtual lines, groups, curves boundaries.	Local surface orientation and discontinuities in depth and in surface orientation	3-D models hierarchically organised in terms of surface and volumetric primitives

Low-level Vision	Luminance Color Spatial freq. Temporal freq. Local Motion	Low-level coding	Mid-level Vision	Textures Surfaces Lighting Global motion Depth	Mid-level coding	High-level vision	Objects Characters Actions Intentions	High-level coding

David Marr, modelling vision,
Vision (1982).

Information visualizations

A site like the IBM-sponsored *Many Eyes* offers a useful suite of tools for turning data sets into the most common visualization types and also provides some basic guidelines for selecting visualizations appropriate to the task at hand. This lively chart is interactive on the web. It shows traditional print graphics alongside computer generated visualizations. Created by Ralph Lengler and Martin Eppler, it provides a clear roadmap for exploration of the world of information visualizations.

Many Eyes, information visualizations.

A periodic table of visualization methods (2007).

Interface design

An interface can show information or it can support tasks and behaviors. Jesse James Garrett's oft-cited chart shows the tensions between these two different approaches to the design of the "user experience." Understanding the trade-offs between information and task-oriented strategies and the implications of picking between them is crucial to effective interface design. Adding humanistic values to the ways interfaces structure critical insight is also essential, allowing for contrast, comparison, and exposure of the act of making meaning rather than simply presenting options on a menu. Humanistic interface is in its infancy, but can build on these precedents.

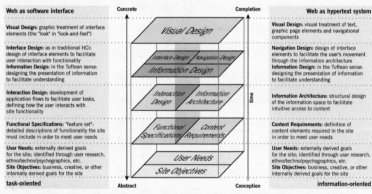

Jesse James Garrett, elements of the user experience (2000).

The "book" of the future

The "book" of the future will combine reading and writing, annotation and social media, text processing and analysis, data mining and mind-mapping, searching and linking, indexing and display, image parsing and distant reading, in a multi-modal, cross-platform, inter-media environment. Pages will be temporary configurations based on calls to repositories and data sets. We will "publish" our data trails as guidebooks for the experience of reading, pointing to milestones and portals for in-depth exploration of stories, inventories, and the rich combination of cultural heritage and social life in a global world. The display will take advantage of the n-dimensional space of the screen in ways that combine multiple design visions.

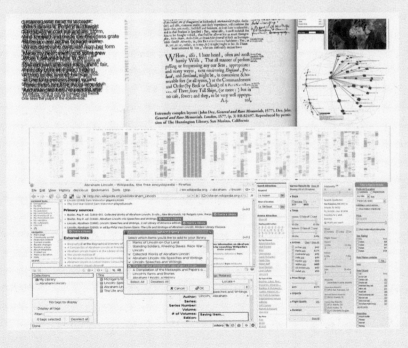

A future multi-modal book.

Interpreting Visualization :: Visualizing Interpretation

Almost all of the formats used in visualizations or information graphics have venerable histories. In this section we look critically at those intellectual lineages. The roots of tables and charts, calendars and timelines, maps and diagrammatic forms are as old as writing and record-keeping. The imprints of the disciplines of origin are still present in the schematic organization according to which these visual forms produce meaning. Some are deeply humanistic in their orientation and use, others more tightly bound to managerial, administrative tasks, or to the empirical tenets of the natural and physical sciences. Making connections between the disciplinary roots and the current uses of visual forms lets us interpret the graphical relations encoded in these familiar images, teasing out from them some analytic principles about the way they work. We are still Babylonians, in our use of the calendar, our measure of days, hours, and minutes, just as we remain classical in our logic, medieval in our classification systems, and modern in our use of measurements expressed in rational form. Each of the many schematic conventions in daily use and the frequently unquestioned appearance in our documents and websites replicate ideologies in graphics.

A basic distinction can be made between visualizations that are *representations* of information already known and those that are *knowledge generators* capable of creating new information through their use. Representations are static in relation to what they show and reference—a bar chart presenting statistics about voting patterns is a good example. Knowledge generators have a dynamic, open-ended relation to what they can provoke; for instance, a train time-table can be used to calculate any number of alternative itineraries. The tension between static representations and dynamic generators will weave through our discussion.

We can also organize our study of the forms of visualization using several different parameters: graphical format (map, table, timeline, tree, bar chart, network diagram), intellectual purpose or function (mapping, navigating, record keeping, calculation), the type of content they express (qualitative, spatial, temporal, quantitative, interpretative), the way they structure meaning (by analogy, connection, comparison, using nodes/lines, vectors, columns, bi- and multivariate

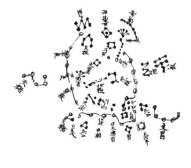

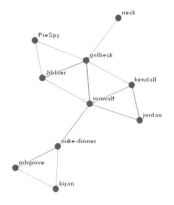

axes, point of view systems, etc.), or their disciplinary origins (bar diagrams from statistics, trees from genealogy, maps from exploration, and flow charts from management or electrical circuits). Many visualization programs give advice about which chart or graph to use based on the kinds of data and relations among variables being graphed.[76]

But however we classify the visualizations we use, they all require the same analytic approach to expose the workings of their graphical organization as meaning-producing. Diagrammatic images spatialize relations in a meaningful way. They make spatial relations meaningful. And they do so according to conventions that embody assumptions about how we translate observation, sensation, perception of phenomena into knowable forms. The interpretative acts that become encoded in graphical formats may disappear from final view in the process, but they are the persistent ghosts in the visual scheme, rhetorical elements of generative artifacts. The challenge is to develop a terminology for the rhetorical iconography of graphical forms that is grounded in the features of spatialized relations such as hierarchy, juxtaposition, and proximity. [See Window 6, information visualizations]

Information visualizations have their origins in record keeping and observation. Timelines, calendars, tables used for accounting purposes are among the oldest formats that come down to us in the conventions on which we draw for informa-

Dunhuang star chart (circa 700 AD).

A basic social networking diagram with nodes and edges.

tion visualization in the current moment.[77] Every calendar system has behind it the lurking shape of ancient observations.[78] Trees and maps are also ancient forms, with venerable pedigrees and hordes of evidence and exemplars.[79]

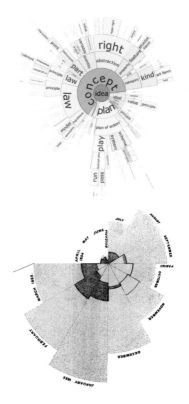

Visualization formats exist independent of particular media. Calendars don't have to be scratched into stone and bar charts don't need to be rendered by engravers with finely tooled burins—any more than scatter plots have to be generated computationally. The increase in availability of means of production and reproduction, and relative ease with which each medium can be used and its multiples put into circulation certainly have an impact on the popularity and quantity of visualizations at different moments. Thus we may cite many instances of diagrams—particularly medical, herbal, astrological, and alchemical—in the manuscripts produced in monastic libraries and Islamic courts in the millennium between the fall of Rome and the fifteenth century development of the printing press. But the development of copperplate engraving supported the flowering of a diagrammatic imagination that embodied late medieval enthusiasm for formal orderings and organizations in visual expressions that were profoundly humanistic in their outlook on knowledge and knowing.

The explosion of visual imagery integral to knowledge production and to exhaustive, extensive attempts at comprehensive presentations of knowledge is intimately bound to

Christopher Collins, Sheelagh Carpendale, and Gerald Penn, "DocuBurst" display of text analysis and data analysis.

Florence Nightingale, diagram of the causes of mortality in the army (1858).

the place of engraving in the publishing industries of the sixteenth and seventeenth centuries. Visuality and knowledge
provided mutual guarantees in the late Renaissance as it met
the early Enlightenment. Diagrams of all kinds migrated
from spheres of intellectual activity as diverse as alchemy,
kabbalistic practice, anatomy, astrology, astronomy, and med-
icine so that we can witness the mapping of one system after
another into bodies, celestial spheres, and other combinatoric
images of hybrid systems.[80] We have only to glance across the
list of influential figures, some concerned with the occult,
such as Robert Fludd, or to others committed to empirical
methods, such as Johannes Kepler, Andreas Vesalius, Galileo,
or Isaac Newton, to understand how quickly and completely
visual forms became essential to intellectual inquiry in the
sixteenth and seventeenth centuries, often without strict distinctions among what we would call "scientific" disciplines
and other systems of belief. In the extensive publishing program of Athanasius Kircher, alone, we witness a dramatic
demonstration of the embrace of visual means as an integral

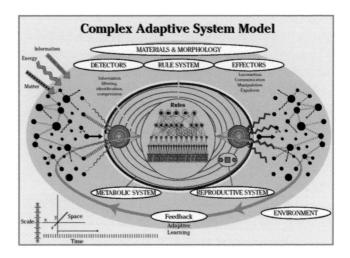

Diagram of a
complex system.

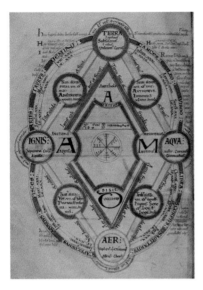

feature of knowledge production and presentation.[81] The diagrammatic imagination of the era is quite fantastic, and the use of figures or analogies as a way to present systematic and schematic information is both graphically and epistemologically stunning. Diagrammatic production surges in the eighteenth century, and the capacities of print production mustered in support were also the instrument through which visual reasoning could be performed in ways that served a rationalizing sensibility committed to the bureaucratic management of the emerging modern state. Whether these alignments were fortuitous or necessary, incidental or causal, hardly matters, since the archive offers a vivid testimonial to the power of statistical thinking and political arithmetic to create graphical conventions in diagrammatic forms.

Bar charts, flow diagrams, scatter plots, and other conventions are of more recent vintage. We find only a handful of anomalous precedents before they come into general use in the final decades of the eighteenth century. However, once they appear in the beautiful plates of Joseph Priestley and William Playfair in the late eighteenth century, they do not appear again in wide circulation for almost half a century.[82] Habits of thought and intellectual fashions are intertwined. The use of diagrams is largely restricted to gridded ta-

Cosmological diagram on vellum from the Book of Byrthferth (circa 1090), St. John's College Library, Oxford, UK.

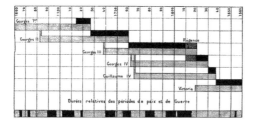

bles in the early decades of the nineteenth century. As I have noted, the diagrammatic character of tables is often overlooked. In the 1830s, when interest in statistics intensified, interest in graphical means of expression revived.[83] A wave of statistical charts and graphs made their appearance in scientific texts and, to a lesser but steadily increasing degree, in works of social or historical analysis. According to historian Michael Friendly, the use of diagrams rises and falls with a late nineteenth century "golden age" in Europe followed by one in the United States in the early twentieth century that drops off dramatically by about 1945. American interest revived steadily into the present, while the Europeans became focused on mathematical, rather than graphical, approaches to statistical analysis.

The fashion for visualization waxes and wanes, and the fortunes of graphs and charts to depict or generate abstract relations among elements (entities or quantities) spike and fall dramatically until the advent of computational systems. Now the ease with which the pie charts and standard timelines can be generated from any and every form of processed information as "data" makes these conventional forms as frequent as pop-up ads, animated banners, and other elements in the graphic landscape of the Web. Often these forms are used without clear understanding of their rhetorical force or the suitability of their underlying semantic structuring principles to the problem for which they supposedly present a solution or transparent analysis. As programs specific to the field of visualization become more sophisticated, so do the aesthetic qualities, as well as the sophistication of informa-

Etienne-Jules Marey, timeline of the reigns of the English monarchs (1885).

tion analysis and knowledge production. The challenge is to break the literalism of representational strategies and engage with innovations in interpretative and inferential modes that augment human cognition.

We will begin this study with a list of formats of visualizations, look to their antecedents and disciplinary origins for some insight into their formal organization as a knowledge scheme, reflect on the operation of their format features, and then engage with some of the contemporary uses and abuses of these visual conventions in current environments. This will begin to show how the relation between interpreting visualizations and creating schemes for visualizing interpretation can proceed.

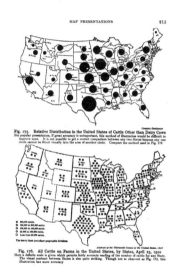

Visualizations and diagrams depend on the same basic graphic principles as other visual sign systems: *the rationalization of a surface* (setting an area or space apart so that it can sustain signification), *the distinction of figure and ground* (as elements of a co-dependent relation of forces and tensions in a graphical field), and *the delimitation of the domain of visual elements so that they function as a relational system* (framing or putting them in relation to a shared reference). Without these basic principles, no graphical system can work.[84] The other graphical aspects gestured at above—the graphic variables, Gestalt principles, diagrammatic elements and their spatial organization—build on these principles.

Willard Cope Brinton, maps with pins and area symbols to show relative quantities; from *Graphic Methods for Presenting Facts* (1919).

Timekeeping

The movement of the stars is readily available to the human eye, and solar and lunar cycles have an enormous impact on human culture, so not surprisingly, the earliest diagrammatic charts derive from observation of the heavens. Like maps and architectural plans, these charts demonstrate a capacity for abstraction. Their diagrammatic character imposes a conventional, schematic order on natural phenomena and then functions as if it were equivalent to the original. The organization of the calendar into a year of approximately 360 days, organized into larger groupings of weeks or months, arises in the ancient Mesopotamian region by about 2100 BCE.[85] Like writing and numeracy, calendar systems also arise independently in most parts

of the world and are usually based on observable solar, lunar, or planetary cycles.[86] We are so accustomed to understanding the heavens as a set of quadrants and coordinates that we barely register these systems or the graphical conventions. The idea of a celestial sphere, with its equal divisions on an ecliptic or meridian, projects a sense of rhythm, order, and regularity onto the flux of temporal change. The very idea of a year becomes reified through familiarity with the form. The astrological and astronomical divisions of the skies get projected onto human experience as a scheme, or reference frame, against which such experience can be understood or measured. Like maps, celestial coordinate systems become a reified intellectual construct, a graphical scheme through which hu-

Babylonian star chart and calendar from the library of Ashurbanipal, Nineveh, inscribed with Assyrian cuneiform (circa 720 BCE).

man beings create a relation to the phenomenal world.

The Romans had a quasi-grid system for marking time in months and days, but our familiar calendar grid is of much later vintage, appearing only well into the age of print.[87] Western calendar grids, with their division of the week into seven days, led or finished by the Sabbath, impose a cycle of beginnings and endings to the flow of time. The seven-day division is a residue of lunar cycles, structuring time according to the waxing, waning, full, and new moons.[88]

Days, months, and years have a source in planetary revolutions and movements—but what is an *hour*? It is not de-

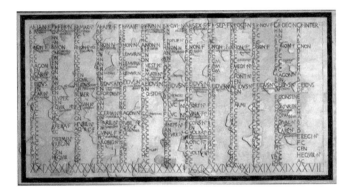

termined by a natural cycle. The structure of hours has no such natural source, and variations in the divisions of time, as well as the identification of the moment of a day's beginning, have varied in ancient and indigenous cultures. We think of days as entities, bounded and discrete, because of our habits of waking and sleeping according to the rising and setting sun. But chunking of time into hourly units has become naturalized by the representations so familiar in our daily use. Such conceits are the result of long habits of shared thought, conventions, or cognitive maps. Any reordering of months into single lines of days—or into other graphical

Calendar of Roman *fasti*, Republican era (84-55 BCE), found at Nero's Villa at Antium, reconstructed by Adriano La Regina (1998).

schemes—strikes us as arbitrary and disorienting. The visual order of the calendar seems like the very structure of time itself, so naturalized has it become through graphic conventions. Like lines on a map demarcating one state or nation from another, the division of one day from another is powerfully structured through graphical conventions. These diagrammatic schemes are *performative*. They make the world by structuring our experience of it.

James Allen and George Ferguson analyzed temporal relations using "interval logic," an abstract set of rules that describe relations that can also

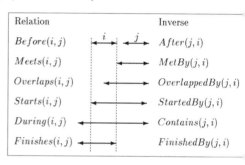

Relation		Inverse
$Before(i, j)$		$After(j, i)$
$Meets(i, j)$		$MetBy(j, i)$
$Overlaps(i, j)$		$OverlappedBy(j, i)$
$Starts(i, j)$		$StartedBy(j, i)$
$During(i, j)$		$Contains(j, i)$
$Finishes(i, j)$		$FinishedBy(j, i)$

be expressed graphically.[89] Their goal was to identify the basic set of possibilities for the ways intervals in time could be related. Their list of primitives is based on assumptions about temporality that might not hold in fiction, imaginative works, or possible worlds scenarios, but apply well to linear, homogeneous, and continuous models of time. So, notions like "branches" or "parallels" are absent from their list of relations, which are descriptions of discrete intervals on a timeline. But the example serves very well to demonstrate that sets of relations that can be described logically or mathematically can also be expressed graphically. We have no difficulty understanding the meaning of "before," "after," or "meets" in the list compiled by Allen and Ferguson.

Some of these logics verge on philosophical investigations—as in the case of attention to the difficult "dividing instant" problem so crucial to computational operations (which side of a divide does a moment separating one task from an-

James Allen and George Ferguson, temporal logic diagram from "Actions and Events in Interval Temporal Logic."

other belong to in an algorithmically initiated process). But these logical approaches do not provide an adequate conceptual framework for humanistic experience of temporal relations. Interpenetrated time, recollection and regret, or even the simple distinction between the time of telling and the time of the told in any narrative do not match the categories offered by the discrete categories of Allen and Ferguson's chart.

Temporal divisions have other ideological underpinnings. A timeline, with its single, linear, homogeneous directional flow, expresses a model of temporality consistent with empirical sciences.[90] But humanistic documents embody many alternative versions of temporality. Humanists deal with the representation of temporality *of* documents (when they were created), *in* documents (narrated, represented, depicted temporality), the construction of temporality *across* documents (the temporality of historical events), and also the shape of temporality that emerges *from* documentary evidence (the shape of an era, a season, a period, or epoch). They need a way to graph and chart temporality in an approach that suits the basic principles of interpretative knowledge.

Conceptions of temporality in humanities documents do not conform to those used in the social and empirical sciences. In empirical sciences, time is understood as continuous, uni-directional, and homogenous. Its metrics are standardized, its direction is irreversible, and it has no breaks, folds, holes, wrinkles, or reworkings. But in the humanities time is frequently understood *and represented* as discontinuous, multi-directional, and variable. Temporal dimensions of humanities artifacts are often expressed in relational terms: before such and such happened, or after a significant event. Retrospection and anticipation factor heavily in humanistic works, and the models of temporality that arise from historical and literary documents include multiple viewpoints. Anticipation, foreshadowing, flashbacks, and other asynchronous segments are a regular part of narratives, and they create alternative branchings, prospective and retrospective approaches to the understanding of events that cannot be shown on empirical timelines.[91]

Human experience of temporality is always relational, thus the marking of epochs in accord with expectations of a messiah's return or in recognition of this as a still-future event mark major distinctions in the Christian and Jewish world views.[92] All of historical time takes its measure in relation to such markers and milestones, and the shape of temporality is an expression of belief, not a chart of standard metrics. The experience of time is highly subjective, as is that of space, and thus the sense of a long moment, a swift day, a fast movie, a slow book requires elasticity in the ways we measure, record, and express temporality. The human record is full of gaps and breaks, ruptures and missing documents, so that any historical reconstruction necessarily provides only partial evidence. Humanistic temporality is broken, discontinuous, partial, fragmented in its fundamental conception and model. How to find the right graphical language to communicate this knowledge in ways that are sufficiently consistent to achieve consensus while being flexible enough to inscribe the inflections that characterize subjective experience?

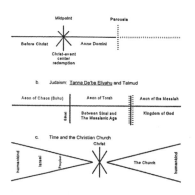

Herbert Bronstein, diagramming time in relation to cultural events; from *Time, Order, Chaos: The study of Time*, James Fraser ed. (Madison, CT: International Universities Press, 1998).

Space-making

Digital mapping often begins with geo-rectification, a task that reconciles spatial data and maps of all kinds with a given standard, such as Google maps or government survey instruments. But the greater intellectual challenge is to create spatial representations without referencing a pre-existing ground. What is the figure of space that emerges from data, observation, experience, human record, when no a priori coordinates are used to structure that representation in advance? Much can be gleaned from early maps, or indigenous presentations of spatial knowledge, that do not follow rationalized conventions of projection.

Early maps served two main purposes: navigation and way-finding, or the identification of ownership and administration of property. Capturing the image of a large landmass within the compass of perception is not part of experiential activity, but requires translation into another system through a complicated series of abstractions, measurements, surveying, compilation, interpolation of quantitative information, representation schemes, and projections. We can see the stars and their relations directly. We cannot "see" the land's shape, its contours, or outlines. The need to navigate contours of the earth and manage its division into property gave rise to mapping techniques in Egypt and Sumeria. An Egyptian map drawn on papyrus dating to 1300 BCE is one of the oldest extant navigational charts, making it younger by more than a millennium than the charts of the heavens tracking movements of the stars. Cadastral maps are early examples of abstraction. They are used to keep track of ownership and property lines and are a feature of the same Near Eastern cultures of Ur and Uruk that produced writing. Wayfinding along a path or across a terrain relies on narrative. A description of a sequence of geographical events based on observation can be transformed into a draw-

Turin papyrus mining map (1160 BCE).

ing of features and landmarks. But abstracting this into a topographic view requires understanding the rationalization of surface and its ordered schemes. Navigation requires both wayfinding narratives and charts based on abstraction. Land management relies more heavily on the representation of geography on a flat surface. City maps were made in Babylonian times, as were plans of architectural spaces.[93] In the opinion of historians of cartography and anthropologists, these represent a significant level of cultural organization.[94]

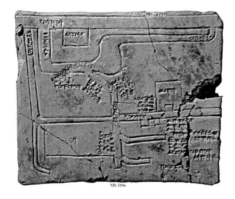

A beautiful cadastral map from 1500 BCE shows a plan of fields in ancient Nippur.[95] Elegantly sketched in clay and inscribed with boundary lines and owners' names, the map is a testimony to the capacity of Babylonian cartographers to perform an act of conceptual abstraction from observation rooted in the experience of the world to a planar representation of it. Six hundred years earlier, someone inscribed a plan for a wall surrounding a large structure, like a temple, onto a tablet on the lap of a stone statue of a prince of Lagash.[96] The drawing may have been used as the plan for construction, or merely to conjure an imagined building, but either way it demonstrates the ability to project a multidimensional form from a flat drawing. These two modes of abstraction—from three-dimensional space to a surface and from a flat plane to an image of projected space—are intellectual activities of a high order that engage their diagrammatic images in a complex social network of administration and planning. They are works that sustain elaborate transactions, both cognitively and culturally. In this case, they derive their structural order

Babylonian clay property map MS 3196, Niru, Babylonia, 22 lines and captions in cuneiform script (1684–1647 BCE).

from existing or projected forms, rather than being abstract diagrams that function without a referent.

The task of mapmaking requires a spatial imagination abstracted from direct observation or experience. In *Making Space,* John Rennie Short describes six distinct "spatial discourses: the construction of the grid; emergence of cosmography; the mappings of the world; the navigation of the oceans; the surveying of the land; and the annexing of colonial territories."[97] To this could be added the earlier acts of narration, description, the records of observation, and journeys. A comprehensive grid system was invented by Ptolemy, the second century Greek-Egyptian working in Alexandria. Complete with longitude and latitude, Ptolemy's system was preserved from antiquity in the work of Arabic scholars, then translated into Latin in the fifteenth century when it came into widespread use.[98] In the medieval period, however, Western cosmography synthesized astronomy, astrology, geography, in a view that put the earth and heavens into a coherent system of spheres and hierarchies. In an era before Ptolemy's system was widely adopted, medieval maps of the known

World map from Claudius Ptolemy's *Geography,* engraved and hand-colored by Johannes Schnitzer (1482).

world took the T-O scheme, the circle of the world (Africa, Asia, Europe) with Jerusalem at the center.[99] The allegorical significance of the form, matching the T of the waters in the shape of a cross with the O of the earth as the bounded globe, aligned with medieval Christianity. While scale and orientation were different from later rational projections or conceptions, the T-O maps were representational, constructed on a visual analogy to the geography familiar to the era. They were symbolic, and fulfilled an expectation that the earth conform to a Christian plan of divine design.

T-O maps were not particularly useful for navigation since they displayed almost no information about the seas, currents, coastlines, or compass points. The invention of the nautical compass and exigencies of the Crusades spawned a new charting system in the thirteenth century known as the "portolano" in which intersection points (later developed

Isidore of Seville's *mapamundi* from his *Etymologies,* written in 623, reprinted by Günther Zainer (Augsburg 1472).

Portolan chart showing navigation routes across the Mediterranean, probably from Genoa (circa 1320-1350).

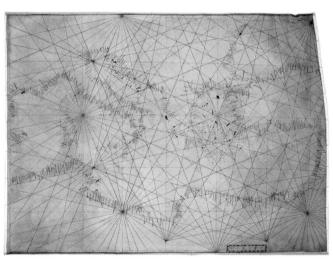

into compass roses) served to orient ships and assist them in charting their course.[100] The imposition of schemes meant to serve particular purposes transformed maps from descriptive to instrumental artifacts, but the

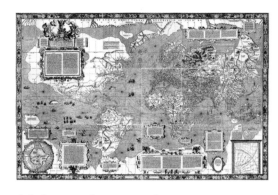

basic approach to mapping global geography remained rooted in Ptolemaic schemes until Gerhard Kremer (known as Mercator) made suggestions for an alternative approach in the sixteenth century.[101] Mercator's rhumb-lines or lines of "constant course" depended on using a consistent linear scale projecting the globe onto a cylinder. The description of the observed world was put into dialogue with graphic systems imposed as abstractions that were not derived from the features of the landscape but imposed upon it through human activity. Advantageous for navigation—Mercator's scheme can be readily translated into directional information—it makes for exaggerations of the size of landmasses at the poles. These distortions are the result of the conceptual abstractions according to which the graphic scheme is conceived. They are convenient conceits, and the rhetorical force of analogy persists. The basic contours of continents and coastlines provide enough familiarity to obscure the abstractions of distorting schemes. Continual corrections and innovative variations of global projection systems continue to this day. Each construction, old or new, is a graphical expression of conventions grounded in historical and cultural exigencies.

Once systematic mathematical means for creating systems of navigation were put into play, "the world was en-

Gerhard Mercator, world map, *Nova et Aucta Orbis Terrae Descriptio ad Usum Navigantium Emendate Accommodata* (1569).

Peter Dicken
and Peter Lloyd,
"The Unevenness
of Time-Space
Convergence,"
*Modern
Western Society*
(NY: Harper
and Row, 1981).

meshed in a grid, laced with compass lines and seen through the lens of the theodolite, back-staff, and cross-staff."[102] The interplay of abstract schemas and concrete reality blurs our understanding, making maps seem "real" though they are elaborate constructions created with allegiance to the conventions of representation as well as expressing a conception of space.[103] Maps depend on a process of "constructing analogies between two-dimensional and three-dimensional space" that "are part of a culture's world view or ontology."[104] After all, "the world itself *has no surface*" experienced by "its manifold inhabitants, journeying along their respective ways of life."[105] Maps, like other graphic conventions, construct normative notions about time, space, and experience that become so familiar we take them for accurate representations rather than constructions. The constructed experience of space cannot be presented in standard cartography any more than the variable concepts of temporality can be charted on a standard timeline.

Spatiality, or the concept that space, like time, is always relational, always produced as a factor of experiential or sub-

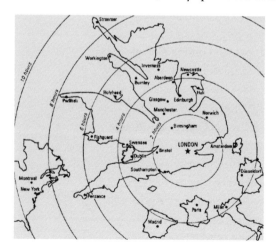

jective effect, is in striking contrast to the empirical concept of space. Mapping depends on projections, of course, but these might take other factors into account as part of the metrics of their design. Francis Galton, for instance, mapped space as a function of subjective observations.[106] Galton's problem, formulated in the mid-nineteenth century,

82

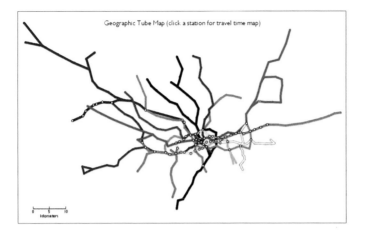

takes into account that most statistical phenomena are observer-dependent and situated, and cannot be separated from the dependencies that bear upon the creation of data. Galton, in other words, recognized that in many circumstances, data were capta. The statistical description of phenomena depend upon the observer's circumstances. A more recent demonstration of these principles is a map designed in 1981 by the team Dicken and Lloyd to show England's geography distorted by travel time.[107] In a related example, designer Tom Carden created a dynamic interface that redraws the London Underground map as a function of time of travel from any selected station to any other station.[108] Another striking example is an early twentieth century map of the United States in which horsepower capacity determines the area of each state though the boundaries and outlines are still recognizable.

Many mathematical forms are diagrammatic in character, and it could be argued that without spatial techniques, mathematical thinking would not have advanced. The sequential ordering of early counting systems occurs in pre-history, where notched bones and other objects provide

Tom Carden, Tube map application that reorganizes the map by time of travel from a particular station.

Pythagorean triplets (length x measure = area), Plimpton 322 clay tablet (circa 1800 BCE), Columbia University, Plimpton Collection.

material evidence of these early experiments. Order, sequence, grouping, size, scale, and placement are signifying features in graphical numbering systems. The Indus Valley civilization of the third millennium BCE (which also gave rise to an indigenous script, which later disappeared) developed place-holding systems, ratio, and other means of controlling proportion, size, and quantity that are spatial as well as quantitative. The sixth century BCE Greek mathematician Pythagoras purportedly travelled to Egypt to absorb the lessons of astronomy, geometry, and other advanced systems that were the combined legacy of ancient learning. Evidence for early Egyptian mathematical activity is sparse, but from Babylonian sources we can trace the development of multiplication and division, as well as simpler computation. These activities are almost impossible to perform without spatial organization in which the numbers hold value through position. Spatial organization in which position confers value underpin many basic mathematical activities from simple calculation to more complex topological concepts. The diagrammatic aspect of basic arithmetic operations tends to disappear in habitual use. We see the numbers as a column in addition, but overlook the implied grid that keeps them bound into meaningful relations. Such organization is an instance of figure/ground relations at

play. The spaces that serve to keep columns separated and figures aligned are not passive or inert. They are active elements supporting crucial tasks of differentiation. The same observation can be made of the features of writing and other notation systems.

Administration and record-keeping

Proto-writing systems that served counting and accounting purposes take shape in the ancient Near East in Sumerian proto-cuneiform around the seventh millennium BCE. By the fourth millennium, the use of well-ordered grid space on clay tablets to separate signs of different types, content, or function demonstrates highly organized graphical principles of organization.[109] Notation and writing systems proper are outside the realm of my discussion here, since their primary purpose is linguistic, rather than graphic.[110]

But as with mathematical forms, the graphical structures that support proto-writing participate in an essential stage of the development of graphical principles.[111] This graphic organization becomes increasingly sophisticated as literacy arises in the ancient Near East. Denise Schmandt-Besserat's study of the relation of pictorial imagery and proto-writing demonstrates the extent to which a ground line essential to the or-

dering of written notation comes to serve a useful purpose in narrative pictorial art.[112] Whether visibly present, as in the case of many Bablyonian tablets and texts, or implied, the ground line is a functional point of reference against which the basic graphic properties of sequence, direction, orientation, size, and scale can register their significance. If the original *trace* complies with logician George Spencer Brown's fundamental *distinction* (as the basis of his *Laws of Form*) and Derridian *différance* (as the originary process of the possibility of signification), then the ground line is the first cognitive *frame*, a *referential boundary*, for putting elements of a

Kish Tablet, from Uruk (3300-3100 BCE) British Museum.

graphical system into relation with each other through a common element. Diagrammatic forms of all kinds are constructed on these bases. The creation of various tabular formats for lists, accounting purposes, and other administrative tasks to which I have been referring in the discussion of mathematics and writing might be the first fully

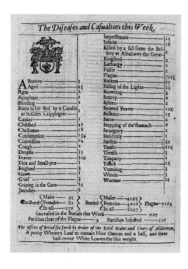

diagrammatic human activity: one in which the spatial distribution of elements creates a structure in support of meaning production, but in which that spatial ordering has no analogical reference or prior existence. The grid format makes its earliest (at least to all current archaeological evidence) appearance in the cuneiform tablets of the late fourth and early third millennia BCE.[113] These were preceded by a series of stages of slowly developing transformations of graphic space in which the signs of quantity and those of specific entities (grain, sheep, etc.) are distinguished from each other by where they are placed on a clay tablet. Groupings, separated by lines, and impressed with respect to alignment and proximity, are all strategies whereby spatial and graphical properties are engaged in a systematic set of relations that help produce meaning. The same signs, in a different order or arrangement, would have different values. The grid is a regular feature of clay and stone tablets by the fourth millennium BCE. The Kish limestone tablet, dated to approximately 3300–3100 BCE, is divided into five distinct zones with vertical and horizontal grid lines.[114] The

Bill of mortality during the Great Plague, Museum of London (Sept. 1665).

horizontal lines are doubled, a gesture that is self-conscious enough to indicate that the lines themselves are not mere conveniences, but play an active part in regulating the signs on the tablet to different roles.

Some visualization formats, such as tables, are so generalizable and re-purposable that their structure almost disappears from view. We take their operations for granted. This graphical organization and its spatial properties carry the trace of the purpose for which a graphic was created. I am not suggesting that this "original" root is some sort of key to semantic value—as if every tree diagram could be reduced to a genealogical meaning. But tree diagrams do share some conceptual commonalities that are structured into the way they use spatial and graphic features that bear the imprint of organic imagery of bloodlines, continuities, derivation, and so on.

Thus the static arrangement of information in a tabular form suggests that it has been modeled according to a strict distinction of content types and that these columns and divisions are neither mutable nor combinatoric. When we con-

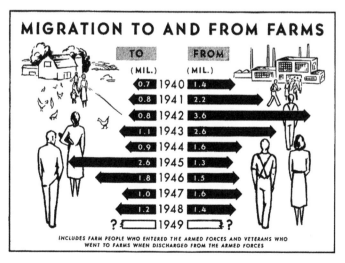

Bar chart showing migration to and from farms, U.S. Bureau of Agricultural Economics Outlook Chart (1950); from Calvin Schmid, *Statistical Graphics* (1983).

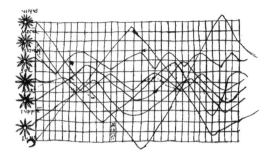

sider the format of an actuarial table or a train timetable, we see that the combinatoric activity it supports necessarily depends on the fixed structure, but that the results generated are a factor of the number of possibilities put into play. The act of reading across and down, through the coordinate grid, to find information is a generative act. A train timetable may present a finite number of options for departure times or arrivals, but making each combination of stations and times generates a result anew. In addition, the information generated engages other non-statistical factors—in particular, the interpretative frame into which these calculated outcomes are put by their human generators. This is not trivial, but essential, to the performative capabilities of tables. They provoke multiple scenarios through their use because the graphic form permits combinatoric variation. Axes are the fundamental spatial elements in graphs, and the allocation of metrics onto the lines that chart variables against each other so that either cross points of intersection or areas between lines (implied or explicit) become charged with value. Sequence and order are constituted spatially as well, and while volvelles and other knowledge generators with movable parts rely on alignment, charts and graphs rely on cross-referencing variables from points on axes into the graphical space. The basic column and row intersections make graphs extremely efficient, but unlike tables, which hold information, graphs and charts make relations among aspects visible according to a set of graphical parameters. Thus selective factors give a powerful rhetorical force to the visualization, and decisions about rela-

Earliest known chart of planetary movements from a translation of Macrobius's commentary on Cicero's *Somnium Scipionis* (tenth century).

tive scale of the (decidedly spatial) metrics on each axis are crucial to the way these relations among elements take shape (literally and intellectually).

Statistical graphs and other modes of data display are intermediate forms between the static format of trees and charts and the dynamic design of knowledge generators, whose designs are capable of giving rise to multiple interpretations or analyses. In the eighteenth century, the science of statistical analysis came into its own with unprecedented force.[115] A few harbingers appeared in the late seventeenth, with the study by John Graunt on the bills of mortality, and the introduction of the term "Political Arithmetic" in a publication by William Petty in the 1670s.[116] The emergence of modern states and the bureaucratic administration for their management drives this development accompanied by the rapid increase of uses of the "Terms of *Number, Weight*, and *Measure*."[117] The purpose of this new approach was to abstract quantitative information from human conditions. All bar charts, line graphs, and scatterplots bear the imprint of that administrative agenda through the assumptions their metrics naturalize in images. Demographics with complex human factors become starkly simplified and reduced graphic statements that conceal as much as they reveal.

Before the seventeenth century, the number of statistical graphs—that is, visual expressions of variables charted against each other as abstract quantities—was extremely small. A rare, and wonderfully innovative image in a

Nicolas Oresme's bar charts, from *Tractatus de latitudinus formarum* (1505).

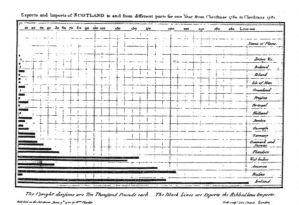

Exports and Imports of SCOTLAND to and from different parts for one Year from Christmas 1780 to Christmas 1781.

The Upright divisions are Ten Thousand Pounds each. The Black Lines are Exports the Ribbed lines Imports.

tenth century manuscript shows the movements of the planets (*De cursu per zodiacum*).[118] The image is an anomaly, and like the mid-fourteenth century plottings of variables and functions by Nicolas Oresme, remains without imitators for more than three hundred years.[119]

The idea of graphical plotting either did not occur, or required too much of an abstraction to conceptualize. For unknown reasons, from 1350 until the late 1600s, no instances of plotting statistical information in graphic form seem to have been put into practice. Tables and charts abound, and so do many variations on tree structures, but no graphs of variables plotted as abstract data.

René Descartes's seventeenth century work in analytical geometry established the mathematical basis for statistical graphs, for which "the principle of coordinates and the idea of functionality" were "sufficient."[120] His creation of a rational grid (grids had been extant, as we have seen, from ancient times) allowed lines and points to serve as key markers on a surface plane. Either could be used as a method of creating a systematic set of graphic relations (either cross-points or intervals or both could carry value). These mathematical means combined with intensifying interest in empirical measurements, but they were only slowly brought together into graphic form. Instruments adequate for gathering "data" in repeatable metrics came into play, as one of the defining elements of modern scientific methods. Thus the eighteenth century astronomer William Herschel charted barometric pressures and temperatures at

William Playfair, bar chart illustrating the exports and imports of Scotland (1780-81).

90

different elevations, but the intellectual means for putting such information into statistical graphs only appeared in fits and starts.[121] Tabular presentation of statistical information remained a mainstay even after the spectacular work of Playfair in the 1780s demonstrated the benefits of "presenting to the eye a figure, the proportions of which correspond with the amount of the sums intended to be expressed."[122] Playfair's brilliance resides in his intellectual accomplishment as well as the elegance of execution.[123] The roots of political arithmetic are in the analysis and management of nation states. The link between statistical tables and bureaucratic administration is historical as well as cultural, and Playfair's innovative presentation of statistical information in a manner that made patterns of imports, exports, commodities, and time frames legible established graphical conventions later banalized by common use. We can easily overlook the leap necessary to abstract data and then give form to its complexities. The bivariate graph, with its inexhaustible capacity to spatialize parameters and put them into relation with each other, is an intellectual product of an era in which rationality could be put at the service of theoretical and practical knowledge. Though our perception of its theoretical sophistication has become dulled through constant use, it allows any two conceptual entities to be put into relation with each other to generate a new result through graphical form.

Primitive graph paper appeared in the 1680s, but commercially prepared gridded sheets were not in production until almost two centuries later.[124] The late eighteenth century work of Playfair and his contemporary, Joseph Priestley, notwithstanding, the use of bar charts and line graphs did not proliferate immediately. The visualization depended on "the dual process of plotting experimental and observational data and of analyzing the resulting graph."[125] Decisions about how statistical parameters are translated into graphics are crucial.[126] The scale of one axis in relation to the other, the use of broken or continuous metrics, decisions about how to sequence and order statistical information, and the rhetorical force of choices about graphic attributes (color, tone, weight of lines) had to develop as a set of conventions; they were not self-evident elements. Each represents a variable that becomes part of the statistical material in visual form. Tonal value, height of bars, or decisions about whether to use bars or curves become part of the value legible in these graphs. In many instnances, eighteenth century elegance degenerated into late nineteenth and early twentieth century crude and clumsy methods.

The intellectual assumptions expressed in bar graphs and pie charts combine empirical and managerial approaches. The basic questions of how parameterization is set up, how samples are taken, and whether curves are presented in smoothed or rough format become instruments of meaning production. Francis Galton's studies of inherited characteristics are classic images in this field, with their well-shaped diagrammatic forms supporting rather too well his eugenic arguments.[127] Their method and format meet a comfortable match, with outliers removed, effaced, eliminated, and the argument made into a hygienic and consumable form. They emphasize the overall curve and obliterate the specifics. The very act of "chunking" dates, quantities, in the abstraction of observation into data, underlies graphical chart making. The width of bars, the height of grids, the proportions of areas created as a result, are the means by which statistics become abstracted from circumstance so that the human conditions may be administered without troubling detail. Here we see the social sciences gain legitimacy through appropriation of supposedly empirical methods, and the presentation of infor-

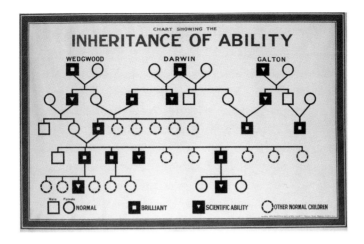

mation in abstracted, deracinated disconnection serves its particular ends with legitimating means.

Florence Nightingale's cockscomb formats were invented to catch attention, to grab the eye, and bring home the real circumstances of hospital conditions for the wounded in the American Civil War.[128] They are presentational, rather than analytic. The area represented in the arcs is not proportional to the quantities they are supposed to represent. But they worked. By contrast, the scatter plot of statistical information that allowed the course of a cholera epidemic to be traced to a single pumping station for water in a quarter of London in 1885 was an analytical instrument.[129] It situated its "data" in a graphical form that had some connection to the information being managed, and the use of points in the plotting scheme was a closer match to the circumstances from which they were derived. Many questions can be raised about what, exactly, these points represent in the lifecycle of the disease and its victims, but the scatterplot approach works well in the presentation of discrete bits of information that can be graphed to reveal a pattern. The conviction that

Francis Galton, English Eugenics Education Society poster with tree diagram of inherited ability (1926), Museum of London 84.1/122.

normative curves could be generated from all human statistics, and that the tribulations of individuals could be subsumed into such neutral and objective seeming diagrams, had as its mission "the calculus of reasonableness for a world of imperfect knowledge."[130] The "knowledge" produced in such diagrammatic displays, filled as they are with the bureaucratic character of managerial sensibility, is already meant for instrumentalization.

Flow charts appeared in the early twentieth century, apparently for the first time in a presentation done by efficiency expert Frank Gilbreth.[131] His 1921 paper to the American Society of Mechanical Engineers, titled "Process Charts—First Steps in Finding the Best Way," is considered the first demonstration of a flow chart. The continued use of flow charts in management and organizational analysis supports the claim that they are well-suited to bureaucratic purposes. Human behaviors and complex situations are reduced to a formalized language of types of information (start points, end points, actions, change moments, input and output, conditionals and decision points). The current codes of activity diagrams and process diagrams is a dramatic example of the ideological imprint of origin on a still-functioning system. The human factors are repressed in these schemes, and the complicated network of interactions is devoid of emotional affect or impact. They are extremely useful for showing work flow, or reducing processes to discrete chunks of activity. They make it easy to impose the will of an administered culture on the complexities of human behaviors.

Area-based visualizations can be created directly from computational methods. Tree-maps, for instance, are based on percentage values. These are presented as solid areas within a whole, their hierarchy expressed through proximity and subdivision of a rectangle. Because these can be generated easily from mathematical processing, they are specific to the environment of digital media. Creating such a diagram by hand requires too many calculations to be feasible. A scatterplot, by contrast, lends itself to hand techniques, since each data point has to be put into place and determining where each point goes is evident on the x-y axes. Scale issues tilt the balance in favor of computational methods, with their automated calculation capacity. Nonetheless, tree-maps depend on several orders of processing—into statistical data, into percentages, and then into a graphic representation—that are readily carried out computationally. A similar point could be made about other visualization formats that take quantitative information into a graphic mode of display that doesn't have any connection to the logical format of the original phenomenon. Tree-maps have no real analogy in the physical world, their spatial divisions are not like those used in cutting cake, dividing a field, allocating space, but are generated automatically through analysis of percentage expressed as a graphic hierarchy dividing a given area in proportion to a quantifiable variable.

Arbor scientiae (Tree of Wisdom), Ramon Llull (Barcelona: Pere Posa, 1505).

Trees of knowledge

Trees of knowledge are graphical forms whose structure is static and fixed, but whose spatial relations carry meaning.[132] Their depiction of hierarchy, derivation, consanguity, proximity, and distance, as well as scale, all participate in the production of meaning. Many databases have a tree structure, as do many forms of structured data and files.

In tree diagrams, the nodes and the

Geoffroy Tory,
Pythagorean Y,
Champfleury
(1525).

branches embody value, their spatial organization structures meaning. A genealogical tree presents an easy example of a venerable form repurposed in digital formats. The generational distinction of father or mother from grandparent, aunts and uncles from children, and first from second and third cousins is structured into the presentation, as are assumptions about bloodlines. The spatial organization of family members tells us about birth order, consanguity, generational breadth and span, as well as patterns of marriage, fertility, and mortality rates. Charts, graphs, and other structures, like trees, are static rather than combinatoric, and use contrast, comparison, sequence, ordering, rates of change, distribution across the plane, bivariate and multi-variate axes, and time axes to show temporal activity or causality. These spatial features are available to knowledge generators and process diagrams as well, though the combinatoric and generative features of these modes are not really part of trees and other static structures.[133]

The image of the tree as an allegorical symbol has, like many motifs of human culture, a history that reaches into antiquity. Images of a tree of life anointed by the gods, as an image of fertility, or as a link between the divine and the earthly realms are found throughout the Mesopotamian region.[134] Both the tree of life and the tree of knowledge play decidedly crucial roles in Old Testament imagery and are pervasive symbols in Judeo-Christian culture. Among the Greeks, Pythagorean tradition included a tree with two life paths, one easy, one difficult, the first a fat branch filled with earthly pleasures and temptations that dropped its climbers into the jaws of hell and the other a slim and thorny branch, leading to an angelic sphere. Pythagorean imagery was readily absorbed into Christian iconography, its diagrammatic and allegorical features overlaid with reductive moral lessons. Little of this imagery would belong in the discussion of diagrams if it were not for the fact that a schematic abstraction of this structure is used for so many intellectual tasks. Trees of knowledge, whether they imitate natural forms in texture and design or merely adopt its nodes and branchings, are graphical structures that produce meaning through spatial arrangement, not only through a persistent allegorical association.

Tree diagrams contain the imprint of their allegorical origins by implying relations of hierarchy, categories, consanguity, derivation, and degrees of proximity. Thickness of limbs carries meaning, though of course many tree diagrams are abstracted into a scheme of lines and branches. As a method of constructing thought, tree diagrams "were widely used by medieval clerics and then by early modern scholars as they sought to explain through them the meaning of the world."[135] When the tree structure is adapted for genealogical purposes, we mark the shift from metaphor to diagram.[136] Once pressed into service of for-

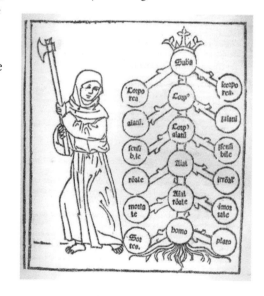

Purchotius, Porphyrian tree from *Institutiones Philosophicae I* (1730).

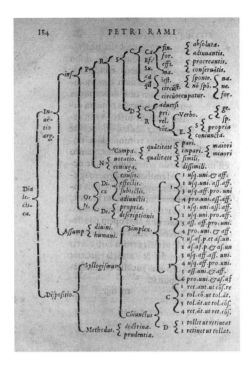

Petrus Ramus, classification structure from *Dialectique* (1555).

mal logic, or conceptual schemes, the tree structure functions in a fully diagrammatic way.

The Porphyrian tree is among the most widespread of these diagrams.[137] The tree is a graphical expression of Aristotle's logical categories, shown as a series of dichotomies along a central branch. The model is simple, powerful, and hierarchal, embodying the neo-Platonic character of Porphyry's influences, Plotinus and Longinus.[138] Porphyrian trees are single, unitary structures whose shape expresses a cosmological hierarchy from highest to lowest being (humankind). The branched pairs at every level of its structure permit a "class" of being and an instance of it to exist in parallel. Questions of universals and their relation to particulars (a priori structure or classification from observation) that divide Platonic and Aristotelian positions are not resolved in Porphyry's organization, but the tree structure could support the projection of logical organizations and classifications of all kinds. The graphical form of the Porphyrian tree is always the same—a trunk serves as the central column of terms, and the branches arranged in perfect bilateral symmetry express the extremes of the central term. The hierarchy moves from crown to roots, with the most abstract and general concept at the top. Thus "Substance," which is the overarching concept in Aristotelian categories, is followed by Body, Animate Body, Animal, and Man.

98

The hierarchy structures a clear value system into the diagrammatic form.

The force of this tree as a descriptive presentation of the Aristotelian categories was so strong that it continued to be the basis of classification systems of all kinds well into the Enlightenment.[139] The binaristic process of division it embodies, founded on a simple act of differentiation (e.g. animate/inanimate) made it adaptable for any systematic ordering based on divisions. These appear in one medieval treatise after another concerned with organizing knowledge in a variety of disciplines. Petrus Ramus, the highly influential sixteenth century French humanist and pedagogue, used the system as the foundation of his method, which in turn gave rise to a whole host of classification schemes in the philosophical and natural sciences.[140] Ramus made a crucial change in visual orientation. He turned the tree on its side so that the classification systems and divisions could run across the page. The single classificatory order could be complemented by a textual order. The alignment of terms follows a columnar organization so that the elaboration of sub-categories forms a clear visual grouping. In essence, this puts both axes (top to bottom, left to right) into play as meaningful. This change calls attention to orientation as a diagrammatic property.

The influence of Ramus's system shows in the "Diagram-

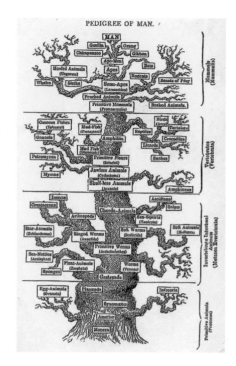

Ernst Haeckel, *Evolution of Man* (1879).

Isidore of Seville, medieval genealogical chart (circa 1160-1165), Bayerische Staatsbibliothek, Munich, clm. 13031.

matic System of Human Knowledge," presented by Denis Diderot at the opening of the *Grande Encyclopedie*. His chart elaborates "a genealogical tree of all the sciences and the arts, marked the origin of each branch of our knowledge, the links they have between them, and the connection to the common stem."[141]

The inflexibility and over-determined relations structured into this format became apparent, however, and between 1750 and 1752, a corrective set in. D'Alembert suggested a cartographic, rather than hierarchical tree format, as a representation of the encyclopedic system.[142] The intellectual implications of a map metaphor replacing a tree image in tables of contents have yet to be played out.

Tree forms can express relationships, not just present a classificatory order. In 1891 Ernst Haeckel's tree of life, a

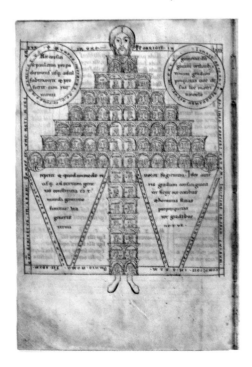

centerpiece to his *General Morphology Based on the Descent Theory*, combined a descriptive classification scheme with a powerful model of derivation.[143] A popularizer and supporter of the work of Charles Darwin, Haeckel drew a fully leafed tree, complete with twists and turns worthy of his talents as an illustrator. With single-celled organisms at its base and men at its crown, the tree imposes a very different order from Porphyry's tree. Far from the world of metaphysics, Haeckel structured his tree to make the evolution of humans from cells into a single continuous process, holistic,

100

organic, and unbroken by leaps or checks in the progress toward humankind. Here the disposition of limbs is strategic, and the placement of *gorillas* and *orangutans* on either side of humankind, but on a branch that stems from a point in the trunk they do not share with their human brethren, is significant. In fact, the juncture points on Haeckel's trunk are the clues to his scheme of the animal kingdom. His is not a simple binary structure. The many branches at each level are bracketed into classifications he marks on the right edge. The passage from protozoans to crustaceans, from amphibians to mammals, appears as smooth as the growth of a single organism.

Haeckel's image is highly rhetorical. The expression of continuity tends to conceal the nodes or decision points that organize its structure. Graphical expediency plays a role as well, so that mollusks are level with echinoderms though their branch peels off at a higher level from the main trunk of the tree. The substitution of the naturalistic tree for the schematic disks and lines of Porphryian structures imposes its force. Though both are classification systems, Haeckel's suggests continuous derivation while the Porphyrian suggests discrete levels that remain separated by the graphic structure in a manner that reinforces their conceptual separations.

Biblical texts traced a lineage of begetting, and an-

Herrad of Hohenburg, Tree of Jesse from *Hortus Deliciarum* (early twelfth century).

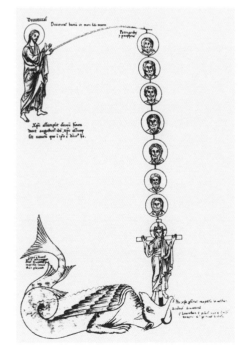

Ramon Llull, tree structure from mss. of *Arbor naturalis et logicalis, Ars Generalis Ultima* (1305).

cestral connections would bring Old and New Testament into alignment with the iconography of the Tree of Jesse. Genealogical trees are of late medieval vintage, not appearing until about 1200.[144] Little in the way of genealogical diagrams exists in antiquity or the early medieval period. Though brought into use around 1300 for justification of royal lineage, "the figure of the genealogical tree as we know it became fully established" only toward the end of the fifteenth century.[145] In medieval scholastic culture, family relations were shown by disks connected with lines, but Arab calligraphers spelled out the names of individuals in bands that connected branches of families, stressing the identity of the link, rather than the autonomy of entities.[146] By the early Renaissance, the lineage of sovereigns, and even of nations, as well as the "organs in the apparatus of the monarchical state" were

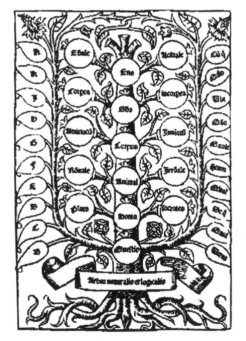

often rendered in arboreal images.[147] Here the ideological message is quite clear in the effect of naturalizing an administrative organization by presenting it as an organic form. The designs produced by Albrecht Durer for a printed image of the triumphal arch of Emperor Maximilian (a project that spanned two years from 1517–18 and was three meters high and made of about 200 woodblocks) might be the single grandest expression of such relations.[148] Genealogical charts reify generational distinctions, making family histories into a series of marked levels, one descended from another, and with members entering the family through marriage often presented without roots or connections.

The more complicated structures of kinship, often necessary for determining royal succession or inheritance, or for the many other matters of anthropological importance, are not able to be fully accommodated in a branching structure of nodes and lines, especially when generations overlap or bloodlines are concealed. Tree-based classification systems assumed common ancestors and direct lineages. DNA mappings often tell a different story, one that contradicts the organic metaphors with their linear narratives of evolution. When these structures are adopted for organizational charts with reporting lines, or data structures in which "inheritance" is a feature, the full force of the ideological effect is in play.

Examples of trees and schemes could be proliferated endlessly, and each, in its structured arrangement, offers the opportunity for examination. If the branches of the Porphyrian structure suggest that the paired branches of its limbs have equal stature, and if trees of consanguity imply an indisputable relation of continuity (and legitimacy), and the adoption of these formats into the structure of classification systems implies that relations of elements in such a system are built on concepts of parent-child inheritance of characteristics of a class, and spheres suggest discrete zones of containment, then what they have in common is that they are fixed, schematic expressions of information in which spatial relations have value.

Network diagrams and topic maps have many features in common with trees, but they are not hierarchical.[149] They

John Major,
logic diagram
(fifteenth century).

have nodes and lines, or points and edges, whose relationship is usually directed. Trees of knowledge almost always express directed graphs whose order cannot be reversed. Just as a biological child cannot become the parent of its parent, so a child in a data structure cannot assume hierarchical dominance over the parent node. In network diagrams the structures are created through tripartite relationships. An entity-relationship-entity model allows the line that connects two elements to have an attribute or character assigned to it. Weight and value, color coding or inflection through other graphic features that distinguish one kind of relation from another, can be readily generated from well-structured data sets. These have the branching structure of trees, but in the case of topic maps, might have variability in their configuration. If any node can become the top node, by selection, and the graph reconfigured around that node, then the hierarchical fixity of the tree structure is transformed. Because directed graphs carry information attributes (e.g., *x knows y*) that are not necessarily determined by a sequence of lived events (e.g., *z is the father of a*), their polarities may be reversed and their order manipulated. The

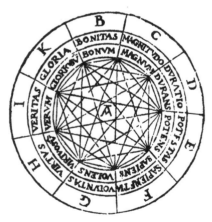

spatial distribution of network diagrams, topic maps, and other graphical expressions of processed text or intellectual content is often determined by the exigencies of screen real estate, rather than by a semantic value inherent in the visualization. This introduces incidental artifacts of visual information. A point in a graph may be far from another because of a parameter in the program that governs display, rather than on account of the weight accorded to the information in the data set. The argument of the graphic may even be counter to the argu-ment of the information, creating an interpreta-tive warp or skew, so that what we see and read is actually a reification of misinformation.

Knowledge generators

Knowledge generators are graphical forms that support combinatoric calculation.[150] Their spatial organization may be static or mobile, but their spatial features allow their compo-nents to be combined in a multiplicity of ways. They make use of position, sequence, order, and comparison across aligned fields as fundamental spatial properties. Train time-tables and Ramon Llull's volvelles are knowledge generators. So, I would suggest, is a list of numbers to be added up, or a problem in long division. The outcome is determined by a set of operations, but the result is a product, generated through the combination of spatial organization and a set of rules for its use. Many instruments for the calculation of times of day, position on the globe, navigation, are knowledge generators. They are taking a fixed set of values and allowing them to be recombined for different uses and purposes. The spatial orga-nization supports the combinations or calculations that pro-duce the result. The values do not change, and no new infor-

Kellogg's Company Wheel of Knowledge (1932).

mation goes into the system in the process of computation, though results are arrived at through the mechanical, dynamic operation of their elements.

At the outset of their classic, *Logical Reasoning with Diagrams*, Jon Barwise and Gerard Allwein state, "A striking feature of diagrammatic reasoning is its dynamic character."[151] Their goal was to study the "logical aspects of reasoning that use non-linguistic forms of representation."[152] Diagrams, clearly, are not surrogates for linguistic statements, nor are they mere representations of formal knowledge already gained. They are generative systems composed of unambiguous elements that can be used to model and articulate proofs.[153]

In a landmark 1987 essay, "Why a Diagram Is (Sometimes) Worth Ten Thousand Words," Herbert Simon and Jill Larkin argue that a diagram is fundamentally computational, and that the graphical distribution of elements in spatial relation to each other supported "perceptual inferences" that could not be properly structured in linear expressions, whether these were linguistic or mathematical.[154] They state at the outset that "a data structure in which information is indexed by two-dimensional location is what we call a diagrammatic representation."[155] They argue that the spatial features of diagrams are directly related to a concept of location, and that location performs certain functions. Locations exercise constraints and express values through relations, whether a machine or human being is processing the instructions. Larkin and Simon were examining computational load and efficiency, so they looked at data representations from the point of view of a three part process: search, recognition, and inference.[156] Their point was that visual organization plays a major role in diagrammatic structures in ways that are unique and specific to these graphical expressions. In particular, they bring certain efficiency into their epistemological operations because the information needed to process information is located "at or near a locality" so that it can be "assessed and processed simultaneously."

By contrast to trees, knowledge generators are combinatoric. In some instances, the generative capacity is effected by moving parts. In others, the diagrammatic form produces multiple outcomes through the reading of variables against each other even though no part literally moves. The combinatoric art of the already noted thirteenth century Catalan philosopher Ramon Llull was based on the use of rotating wheels. In 1275, Llull designed his first major treatise, *Ars Generalis Ultima*, published in 1305 as *Ars Magna*.[157] His system consisted of lists of the attributes of God, and all the possible connections between them, virtues of the divine creator, and other exhaustive, formalized systems for contemplating and meditating upon theological points. Martin Gardner summarizes Llull's method succinctly: "In every branch of knowledge, he believed, there are a small number of simple basic principles or categories that must be assumed without question. By exhausting all possible combinations of these categories we are able to explore all the knowledge that can be understood by our finite minds."[158] Thus tables of combinations and concentric volvelles produced all possible permutations through multiple rotations. Llull used the term *camera*, meaning room, to indicate the divisions of space on his wheels, suggesting they were containers of value, not just conveniences or labels. If we are to study the attributes of god, we can rotate a volvelle to find that his patience is eternal, his glory just, and his wisdom truth. Fixed entities on stable structure allow for realignment as an effect of their graphical structure. Not all his diagrams were so affirmative, and the states of the soul allowed for forgetting, abnormal hatred, and other negative combinations.[159] The combinations of virtues and sins gave advice, offering appropriate responses or conditions for anger or patience. The set of combinatoric wheels governing relations between things put abstractions and qualities into play: beginning, end, affirmation, negation, doubt, similarity, contrariety. All were distributed in accord with a system of triangular pointers and pivoting disks which had value in each and every of the many extensive possible combinations. Llull's is a generative system, not a representation.

Like astrolabes, nocturnals, and other devices for calculating time, position, or direction in celestial observation and navigation, Llull's circular elements pivoted around a central point to produce their multiple combinations. Arabic philosophers used a device called a *zairja* that used the 28 letters of the Arabic alphabet to calculate new ideas along similar lines. Other combinatoric uses of rotating devices appear in astronomical studies, allowing the positions of stars to be forecast. The late medieval imagination engaged in elaborate diagrammatic invention in the design of charts, instruments, and devices that could be used to chart the heavens.[160]

Though Ramon Llull is regarded by some as a predecessor to modern computing, his mechanical calculators are rigid in graphical form.[161] Their fixed formats only support limited permutation, and though their formal structure can be adopted for many different values, the method remains mechanistic and limited in the generative activity of its outcome. Volvelles were adaptable. The 1564 edition of another late medieval work, Petrus Apianus's *Cosmographicus Liber*

Gottfried Leibniz, *characteristica universalis* frontispiece to *Dissertatio de Arte Combinatoria* (1666).

(updated by Gemma Frisius), makes use of volvelles to more naturalistic ends, for calculation of the movements of planets, calendars, and the like.[162] An extremely popular work from its initial publication in 1524 through the end of the sixteenth century, Apianus's text served as a reference work on astronomical, navigational, geographic, and other matters. The simple device of revolving circles as a generative instrument was readily disconnected from philosophical and mystical realms. The simple principles of rotation and alignment, spacing and metrics along a circumference, are powerful spatial elements that sustain combinatoric activity. The design of volvelles, rotating wheels, can be put to many purposes.

Leibniz's *Dissertatio de arte combinatoria*, published in 1666, absorbs the lessons of Llull into a dialogue with Descartes's idea of an alphabet of reason grounded in *mathesis*.[163] Descartes's coordinate system had made a crucial step by allowing geometrical forms to be represented algebraically and graphed. The focus of Leibniz's search—for a universal calculus that would demonstrate the way the four basic elements gave rise to all other objects in the world—shows how much the late medieval cosmologies still held sway. The diagram drawn by Leibniz for the 1666 publication seems a world away from the approaches to logical syllogisms that fill his notebook pages.[164] When put next to his "stepped reckoner," a mechanical device that exhibits its modernity through the rational workings of its design, the diagrams for his *arte combinatoria* seem like peculiar anachronistic vestiges of a kabbalistic sensibility.[165] The "reckoner," like other mechanical devices mentioned above, used for specific purposes (celestial, navigational, or time-keeping) was a knowledge generator in built form. The relation of this device to the combinatoric format of diagrams is obvious, and the extension of the principles of a system of elements put into combinatoric play

Gottfried Leibniz, manuscript analyzing syllogisms (late seventeenth century).

is what makes them effective for calculations. Leibniz's combinatoric sensibility led him into the study of binary arithmetic, and his discovery of the *I Ching*, with its hexagrams of solid and broken lines, confirmed the power of the system as both a universally symbolic and cosmologically generative one.[166] The *I Ching* is a powerful combinatoric system. Leibniz was attracted to its simplicity (the lines work as a set of binary combinations of broken and unbroken, stable and changing elements in all sixty-four possible combinations of two trigrams) and its claims to be complete.

The squares of opposition prevalent in medieval logic were first described by Aristotle in *De Interpretatione*.[167] The earliest graphical instance seems to come in a second century manuscript of Boethius.[168] The arrangement of four terms in relations as contradictory and contrary allows combinatoric contemplation and discussion. They can be used to express

any set of terms to be put into productive tension. Their simplicity supports a highly generative set of relations, since each of the terms is connected with the others and the mind contemplates these alternative arrangements as an intellectual exercise. In short, they provide a performance of probable interpretations. The square with its four nodes and crossings can be extended with additional nodes and connecting lines, but the dynamic tensions generated by the combinatoric structure are present even in the simplest versions. In hyperbolic examples, the lines of relation, each labeled and carefully interlaced, can track an entire field of dynamic interplay. Another object of contemplation, the Sephirotic Tree, is an outgrowth of twelfth and thirteenth century Kabbalah, a set of Jewish mystical practices.[169] The Sephirotic Tree is a chart of emanations, made concrete in cosmic creation. The central axis is deemed neutral, the outer ranks designated as conduits of active and passive energy. The mystical practice of contemplation was meant to bring the soul into holistic relation with God through engagement with the movement of spiritual energy through the sephirot. Allegorical images from the late medieval period abound in Renaissance emblem books, and the symbolism of the Tarot, astrological signs, and many occult practices. But the Sephirotic Tree is distinct among these other images by virtue of being diagrammatic—the shape of its organization and the intellectual structure it represents are the same. Its generative potential is spiritual knowledge, rather than rational or intellectual insight. As such, it is representative of diagrams used in esoteric and mystical practice, such as magic squares and other configurations. Its workings are combinatoric, the mind must move through its structure to engage.

Graphic tables were used to solve computational problems from the time of Hipparchus, and graphical systems for calculating logarithms had been made into working instruments in the seventeenth century. Descartes developed his

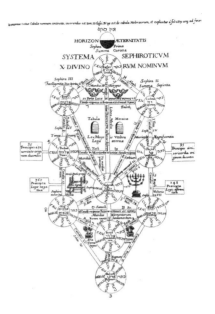

Athanasius Kircher, Sephirotic Tree, *Oedipus Aegyptiacus* (1652-1654).

analytical geometry as a "means for the general graphic representation of laws and formulas by aid of two axes at right angles."[170] These are generative graphic techniques. Another such instance is the contribution made by the eighteenth century mathematician Leonhard Euler who created a method of using circles in intersecting and enclosing relations to demonstrate syllogistic principles, sets, and their relationships. These are similar to the diagrams of John Venn, familiar from set theory, created in the late nineteenth century, though the two systems differ in their particulars.[171] Each is a graphical means of resolving syllogistic questions, and determining an outcome about sets and relations through graphical means. Euler worked on graph theory, calculus, and topological problems that had graphical counterparts. The diagrammatic methods and formal logic in Venn diagrams are not isomorphic to their arguments—any "set" can be represented by a circle so that its intersection with another set can be graphed. But the information itself need not have anything to do with circular forms or formats.

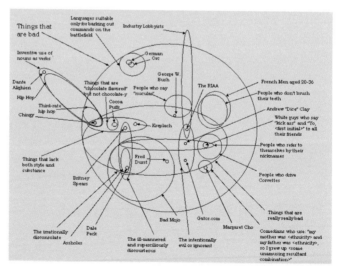

Venn diagram utilized to display behaviors.

By contrast, other graphical systems for the analysis of propositional calculus or solving problems in formal logic generate specifically visual solutions to mathematical problems.[172] For instance, in the late nineteenth century graphical systems for solving calculus problems were developed that became standard in training engineers. The use of specific methods of making curves, plotting intersections, graphing functions, and arriving at a result with graphical methods stayed in use until the advent of digital computers. The complexities of ballistics problems led to development of graphic calculating scales in the early nineteenth century.[173] *Abacs*, or graphic methods of computing, were in common use for designing roads and bridges.[174] Nomography, the system of using graphical calculating devices, makes use of specialized systems of coordinates to create instruments that can compute a mathematical function.[175] The point? Diagrammatic methods of generating knowledge have been integral to mathematics in many varied and subtle ways—the tabular underpinnings of arithmetical operations—as well as more evident ones—set theory, calculus, topology, network theory, vectors, and other fields in which solutions to complex problems may be arrived at through graphical means.

The discussion of knowledge generators and logical graphs would be incomplete without mention of Charles

NOTATION
- Conjunction ("And")
- ⊃ Implication ("If ___ then ___")
- ∨ Disjunction, alternation ("Either ___ or ___or both")
- ⩣ Exclusive disjunction, non-equivalence ("Either ___ or ___but not both")
- ≡ Equivalence ("If and only if___ then ___")
- | Non-conjunction ("Not both ___ and ___")
- ~ Negation ("Not")

BINARY RELATION		NEGATION	
A ⊃ B	If A is true, then B is true	A•~B	A is true and B is false
B ⊃ A	If B is true, then A is true	B•~A	B is true and A is false
A ∨ B	Either A or B is true, or both	~A•~B	Both A and B are false
A ⩣ B	Either A or B is true, but not both	A ≡ B	If and only if A is true, B is true
A	B	A and B cannot both be true	A•B	Both A and B are true
A ≡ B	If and only if A is true, B is true	A ⩣ B	Either A or B is true, but not both
A•B	Both A and B are true	A	B	A and B cannot both be true

John Venn, diagram used to show behaviors, *Symbolic Logic* (1894).

Sanders Peirce and his existential graphs.[176] Venn's work in symbolic logic, first published in 1881, introduced his diagrams. But as Peirce observed, these lacked "iconicity" and were limited in what they could do. Interest in topological relations—spatialized mathematics that is the foundation of network theory—is generally traced to Leonhard Euler's 1736 solution to the Königsberg bridge problem (a problem in routing), but Leibniz had expressed the need for a graphical system of mathematics to address complex geometrical problems more than half a century earlier.[177] The term topology first appears in the 1840s when mathematicians Moebius and Reimann, among others, become interested in connectivity of surfaces as spatial-graphical and mathematical problems.[178] Soon after, Enrico Betti broke away from standard Euclidean understandings of space and introduced the concept of n-dimensional spaces that could only be described mathematically. Set theory and topology are close correlates, and Venn's simple but powerful diagrams used a flat plane that had no metrical features, taking advantage of the simple facts of intersection, area, inclusion, and exclusion.

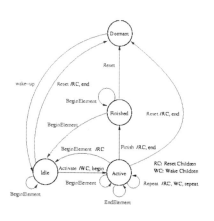

These graphical principles also provided the basis of Peirce's systems. Intent on developing his existential graphs, Peirce envisioned an entire system of graphical reasoning.[179] Peirce's graphical system was a method of logical expression, but also, a means of making logical proofs. He had three systems—alpha, beta, and gamma—each of which had its own rules and constraints. Peirce developed his graphical systems

Charles Gordon, state transition diagram.

114

from a conviction that the linear notation using informal logic was inadequate to the semiotic theories he was formulating in the 1870s and 1880s. The philosophical motivation for the graphical system Peirce invented sprang in part from inspiration by George Boole's *calculus ratiocinator* and its potential to support multiple interpretations. Though largely ignored by his contemporaries, Boole's 1854 *Laws of Thought* put forth a symbolic method from which modern computational procedures are drawn. Like Boole, Peirce considered "logical language as a re-interpretable calculus."[180] Peirce was convinced that reasoning itself was diagrammatic. He distinguished diagrams from figures, saying they were "closer to a unit of a system equipped with representational input and its own transformational rules." Diagrammatic reasoning, he insisted, must be carried out through such a visual, spatial system. The existential graphs were the result of this conviction, the means and site of diagrammatic reasoning. Symbols in a diagram could "be manipulated to obtain other relations."[181] Peirce's project remained unfinished, but aimed at graphing a complete system of relations among existing entities. The graphical vocabulary of his "diagrammatic syntax" consisted of simple but powerful elements, such as inclusion and exclusion, that could be combined according to sophisticated logical rules. The diagrams *performed* the act of reasoning, they did not *represent* it after the fact but were the means of making the logical processes work.

The semantic web makes use of node and line structures that make connections without hierarchy. Webs, like lattice and matrix

Charles Sanders Peirce, existential graphs.

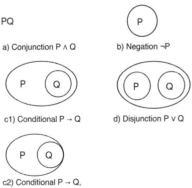

PQ

a) Conjunction P ∧ Q

b) Negation ¬P

c1) Conditional P → Q

d) Disjunction P v Q

c2) Conditional P → Q, alternative notation

formats, are inherently non-hierarchical, with proximity and connectivity relations serving a more powerful rhetorical purpose. Like any two-dimensional surface, a screen can support the illusion of depth using a third axis, particularly useful for graphing events or time-based media like film, video, and audio. Each additional dimension adds complexity. Node-link diagrams support pathfinding, connections, through adjacency and associational trails. In diagrams that need to support multiple paths, even overlapping paths, such as those that display transportation systems (where some lines or roads pass over or under each other rather than intersecting), multiple layered matrices are better suited to the schematic organization of the information than flat diagrams.[182]

Dynamic systems

The combinatoric generators we have been describing can be used to reorganize relations among elements, but they do not change either the elements or the structure that contains them in that process. Diagrams of dynamic events or processes are also generative, but they often display processes rather than products.[183] They use dynamic elements, such as vectors, or directed graph lines, direction, flow, movement, and rates of change as components whose spatial order creates a graphical field. A diagrammatic event is a means of provoking and sustaining processes that are in flux, unfinished, open-ended, complex, or probabilistic. Diagrams of dynamic processes are different from knowledge generators. They are not meant to produce an outcome that can be repeated, or guaranteed by the careful observation of rules (as in calculating scale changes with a ruler or adding a sum of numbers). Instead these diagrams make use of graphical organizations, operations, and relations to analyze or model events or processes. Diagrams of complex systems model many possibilities and probabilities. Values change as the diagrammatic activity progresses, and multiple variables may be active at different scales and rates of change so that the outcome for such a dynamic system is necessarily probabilistic.

New challenges arise in using graphical means to show dynamic processes and events, including complex adaptive systems. Because an event is a state change, a presentation of dynamic circumstances, conditions in which various force, vectors, flows, pressures, or other changeable phenomena are being charted, it does not necessarily lend itself to graphical format. Nonetheless, visualizations of fluid dynamic systems—such as the weather, tides, and atmosphere—have a much longer history on which we can draw. Once again, we can trace literary references into antiquity. Among the Greeks, Thales and others described weather phenomena but creating graphic techniques for meteorological analysis was slower. Aristotelians charted the four elements—earth, air, fire, water—in a diagram that was meant to be generative, productive, capable of the infinite variety of combinations that produced the natural world.[184] This system was frequently refined to show the zones of frigid, torrid, and temperate air, and to indicate the power of the winds to blow from each direction and formed, as we have seen, the basis of Leibniz's view in the 1660s. The effort to align weather changes with planetary movements also gave rise to an industry of observations and calculations. The astronomer Tycho Brahe was convinced that weather forecasting could be done based on astronomical observation.[185] The efforts of the sixteenth century astronomer were copied in later years by figures like John Goad, who recorded thirty years of observations in his 1686 publication, *Astrometeorologica*, tracing the "Discourses of the Bodies Celestial, their nature and influences, discovered from the variety of the Alterations of the Air [...]."[186]

The aforementioned Fludd produced a remarkable image of Meteorology (1626) that combines occult and astronomical imagery. His system allegorizes natural phenomena and allows for the Twelve Winds to be interspersed with images of the Four Archangels.[187] Though mechanistic, his vision of interlocking wheels and spheres hints at dynamic representations of processes and forces.[188] His weather scene is theatrical, and combinatoric, a stage on which diagrammatic play can be enacted by calling the selective elements into play. What it lacks in scientific accuracy it makes up for in imagination.

Diagrams of wind and currents became a feature of navigational maps (Leonardo had done detailed studies of waves and currents, vortices, and other formations in moving water), and seemed to belong to the world of things, observ-

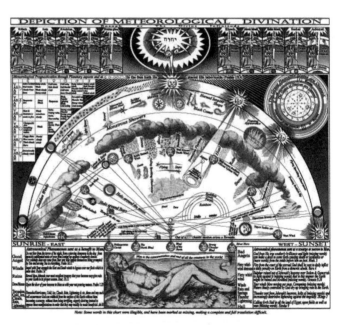

Robert Fludd, *Philosophia sacra et vere christiana seu meteorologica cosmica* (Frankfurt: T. de Bry, 1626).

able, and tractable. But the motions of air, vapor, clouds, and the actions of the atmosphere were more difficult to describe in graphical form. René Descartes's 1637 *Discourse on Method* contains several diagrams that chart processes of atmospheric transformation.[189] These are fascinating, since they are visual attempts to show activities that are almost unseen. Descartes still imagines the world to be composed of the primal elements—earth, air, fire, and water—but his scientific imagination addresses the particulars of molecular structure and operation. Molecules of water, he suggests, are shaped with wiggly tales, small and slippery, so that they can move in between the hard-edged and larger molecules of wood, earth, or stone. These materials are composed of molecules whose edges catch and lock together, but are large enough that water can sometimes still find its way into the crevices left in the interlocking structures. His analyses of rising water vapor, cloud formation, and changes in temperature, early attempts to show complex processes, are unique in their connection of atmospheric activity and landmass. He recognizes that what he is observing and describing is a system, not isolated entities. The lines of pressure and change align directionally, become compressed, and make

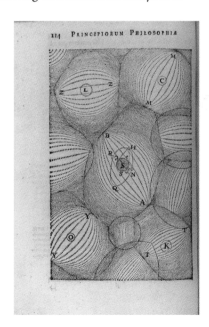

René Descartes, images of meteorological phenomena from *Discourse on Method: Dioptrics, Meterology, and Geometry* (1637).

use of other innovative visual means. Static images, they optimized their graphic capacity to show the thermal and pressure systems in relations of land and air.

Descartes also created a remarkable diagram of energy vortices in the plenum, showing the substance that fills the voids of the universe. The image has a magical dimension to it, presenting the imagined force fields exerted by planets in a pulsing field of activity.[190]

Meteorological observation took a leap with the development of instruments for gauging wind velocity, temperature, and barometric pressure, thus creating a statistical foundation for the science.[191] The thermoscope, invented by Galileo in the last years of the sixteenth century, was soon succeeded by thermometers and barometers capable of regular and reliable readings. Statistical metrics were becoming standardized in this period. Abstracting intangible, sometimes invisible, phenomena into a graphical language and diagrammatic form depended on the intersection of adequate instrumentation and measure, sufficient record keeping to supply data, mapping techniques on which the information could be projected, and then a graphical language for diagramming ephemeral phenomena—or, at least, making a study of the forces and variables of a highly complex system. While meteorological observation forms one excellent case study, the attempt to depict magnetism and other unseen forces was another area in which dynamic processes sought

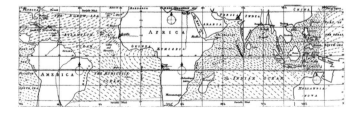

Edmond Halley, map of the winds (1686).

graphical expression as a foundation for understanding. Basic instruments for taking temperature and barometric pressure readings, recording wind direction and, to a limited extent, velocity, as well as precipitation gauges, were chiefly seventeenth century inventions. Edmond Halley is credited with creating the first meteorological chart when he mapped the winds on the surface of the globe in 1686.[192] His arrows of wind direction are not systematic, but they do indicate unstable, changeable conditions. The combination of direction and force is intuitive, but systematic creation of what are known as surface analysis maps only emerged after development of coordinated telecommunications systems. Records of meteorological data started to be mapped in the early nineteenth century, though tides and currents had been charted several centuries earlier. The creation of isobars (lines connecting areas of similar barometric pressure) is attributed to the French meteorologist Edme Hippolyte Marie-Davy in the 1860s, though a map with isobars appears in the 1834 treatise on meteorology written by William Prout.[193]

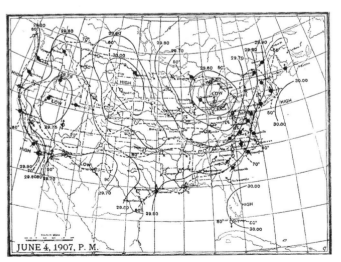

June 4, 1907 thunderstorm mapped using standard conventions with isobars (early twentieth century) from Sverre Peterssen, *Introduction to Meteorology* (1941).

One of a storm in New England in the late nineteenth century shows the graphical system for wind direction and force, isobars, temperatures, and pressure in place. Snapshots of particular moments, they imply process and change rather than actually showing it.

Interest in the microlevel of analysis of meteorological events, long expressed in passages of poetic prose description, found graphical expression in several detailed studies produced in the 1860s. H.W. Dove's *The Law of Storms*, published in 1862, is filled with detailed and technical discussion of measurements of barometric pressure, temperature, wind velocity, and direction as well as storm tracks and wind shifts, even as its title aligns it with the systematic approach to thinking characteristic of other approaches to knowledge and its representation at which we have already glanced.[194] Rear Admiral Fitz Roy's 1863 *The Weather Book* contained carefully mapped meteorological data for several days running that showed the wind directions, velocities, precipitation, temperature, and barometric pressures during a major storm in October 1859.[195] Two years later, Francis Galton's *Meteorographica, or methods of mapping the weather*, created a system of conventions for showing meteorological conditions in Europe for the entire month of December 1861.[196] Methods of showing fronts, precipitation, using isobars, and mapping other data were quickly adopted. The military interest in weather forecasting intensified the pace at which conventions were pressed into use. More sophisticated methods of measuring, including balloons and other devices, combined with simultaneous coordination of information across distances, gave rise to the modern weather map by the late nineteenth century.

Much more could be detailed in the history of graphical representation of fluid dynamics, as increasing sophistication of instruments combined with improved methods of calculation so that rapidly changing conditions, graphed temperature, pressure, and wind conditions became part of forecasting and analysis.[197] But challenges arose from studying thermodynamic properties of the atmosphere whose complexity was just glimpsed by nineteenth century scientists. Non-linear systems posed mathematical challenges. For purposes of thinking about the visualization of interpretation, approaches to the thermodynamics of the atmosphere offer an example of ways an enormous number and type of variables can be put into a model for analysis to generate outcomes that cannot be predicted mechanistically. These systems are extremely sensitive to start conditions, and exhibit emergent behaviors. By the early twentieth century, meteorologists were not only recording observable phenomena (wind, temperature, etc.) but also modeling dynamic systems.[198] The combination of motion graphics, simulation, and computational capability necessary for visualization of complex mathematical models has only been possible with digital computers.

Graphical means in two dimensions, or even the third and fourth dimensions created as spatial-temporal illusions,

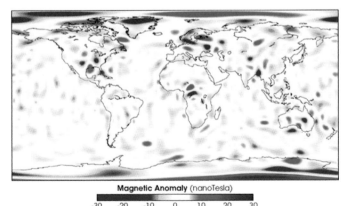

Magnetic Anomaly (nanoTesla)

-30   -20   -10   0   10   20   30

Magnetic activity visualized, NASA.

are often inadequate to address the mathematical complexities involved. But conceptually, we can imagine diagrams of systems with variable organization, changes of scale, and almost inexhaustible complexity in micro to macro modeling. The foundations of chaos and complexity theory arose from the observations of Edward Lorenz, a meteorologist and mathematician, while watching the dynamics of cloud formation.[199] If we are to model interpretation with all of the many variables, statistical and probabilistic distributions it involves, these are the sources to which we will have to turn, even for a speculative vision.

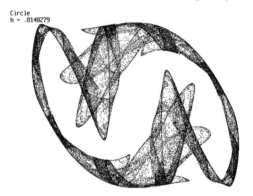

Circle
h = .8140279

Lorenz's engagement with chaos theory resulted in the production of standard diagrams to show the ways tipping points and other events transform the dynamics of systems. Related to chaos theory in its dynamic unfolding, complexity theory uses non-predictive modelling to study probabilistic outcomes of variables in relation to each other within a system as it changes over time. Chaos models show transformation, they are built on interactive variables in a co-dependent, adaptive system, rather than mechanistic models. Dynamic systems, in which adaptation and emergence occur, cannot be graphed in advance. A model has to run its course in order for the outcome to become apparent, and in the process, graphical forms and expressions allow the emerging patterns to become legible. Knowledge is generated, and expressed graphically, but the graphical system is not the means of data input in either chaos or complex systems.

Euler circle,
chaos diagram.

124

Visualizing uncertainty and interpretative cartography

T. Zuk, S. Carpendale, and W.E. Glanzman, "Visualizing Temporal Uncertainty in 3d Virtual Reconstructions," *Proceedings of the 6th International Symposium on Virtual Reality* (2005): 99-106.

Most, if not all, of the visualizations adopted by humanists, such as GIS mapping, graphs, and charts, were developed in other disciplines. These graphical tools are a kind of intellectual Trojan horse, a vehicle through which assumptions about what constitutes information swarm with potent force. These assumptions are cloaked in a rhetoric taken wholesale from the techniques of the empirical sciences that conceals their epistemological biases under a guise of familiarity. So naturalized are the maps and bar charts generated from spread sheets that they pass as unquestioned representations of "what is." This is the hallmark of realist models of knowledge and needs to be subjected to a radical critique to return the humanistic tenets of constructedness and interpretation to the fore. Realist approaches depend above all upon an idea that phenomena are *observer-independent* and can be characterized as *data*. Data pass themselves off as mere descriptions of a priori conditions. Rendering *observation* (the act of creating a statistical, empirical, or subjective account or image) as if it were *the same as the phenomena observed* collapses the critical distance between the phenomenal world and its interpretation, undoing the concept of interpretation on which humanistic knowledge production is based. We know this.

But we seem ready and eager to suspend critical judgment in a rush to visualization. At the very least, humanists beginning to play at the intersection of statistics and graphics ought to take a detour through the substantial discussions of the sociology of knowledge and its critical discussion of realist models of data gathering.[200] At best, we need to take on the challenge of developing graphical expressions rooted in and appropriate to interpretative activity.

Because realist approaches to visualization assume transparency and equivalence, as if the phenomenal world were self-evident and the apprehension of it a mere mechanical task, they are fundamentally at odds with approaches to humanities scholarship premised on constructivist principles. I would argue that even for realist models, those that presume an observer-independent reality available to description, the methods of presenting ambiguity and uncertainty in more nuanced terms would be useful. Some significant progress is being made in visualizing uncertainty in data models for GIS, decision-making, archaeological research, and other domains.[201] But an important distinction needs to be clear from the outset: the task of representing ambiguity

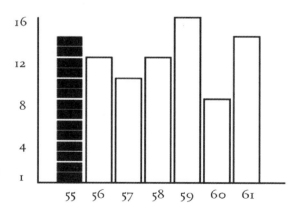

Standard bar chart based on discrete data entities.

and uncertainty has to be distinguished from a second task —that of using ambiguity and uncertainty as the basis on which a representation is constructed. This is the difference between putting many kinds of points on a map to show degrees of certainty by shades of color, degrees of crispness, transparency, etc., and creating a map whose basic coordinate grid is constructed *as an effect* of these ambiguities. In the first instance, we have a standard map with a nuanced symbol set. In the second, we create a non-standard map that expresses the constructedness of space. Both rely on rethinking our approach to visualization and the assumptions that underpin it.

If I set up a bar chart or graph, my first act is to draw a set of one or more axes and divide them into units. The conventional forms of the graphical display of information, "data," make use of a formal, unambiguous system of standard metrics. Charts use simple (if often misleading) geometric forms that lend themselves to legible comparison of values, proportions, or the exhibition of state changes across time. Lines, bars, columns, and pie charts are the common and familiar forms. They render *quantitative* relations with a transparency that seems natural, so that, for instance, if we look at the

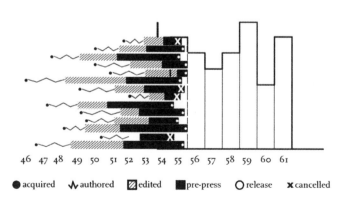

46 47 48 49 50 51 52 53 54 55 56 57 58 59 60 61

● acquired   〜 authored   ▨ edited   ■ pre-press   ○ release   ✕ cancelled

Alternative to standard bar chart showing greater complexity.

127

changes in population across a series of years for a particular location, we can simply accept that from one year to the next rises or drops occurred in the numbers of persons alive in X city in X country at X time. A pie chart showing percentage of resource allocation from national budgets seems completely transparent, self-evident even. A bar chart could compare daylight hours at different latitudes, or the average size of men and women in different countries, or the number of hospital beds in different institutions in a single geographical location and not raise a skeptical eyebrow. But the rendering of statistical information into graphical form gives it a simplicity and legibility that hides every aspect of the original interpretative framework on which the statistical data were constructed. The graphical force conceals what the statistician knows very well—that no "data" pre-exist their parameterization. *Data are capta*, taken not given, constructed as an interpretation of the phenomenal world, not inherent in it.

To expose the constructedness of data as capta a number of systematic changes have to be applied to the creation of graphical displays. That is the foundation and purpose of a *humanistic approach* to the qualitative display of graphical information. That last formulation should be read carefully, *humanistic approach* means that the premises are rooted in the recognition of the *interpretative* nature of knowledge, that the *display* itself is conceived to *embody qualitative ex-*

Steve Smith,
immersive data
visualization.

pressions, and that the *information* is understood as *graphically constituted.* Each of these factors contains an explicit critique of assumptions in the conventional "visual display of quantitative information" that is the common currency. The basic categories of supposedly quantitative information, the fundamental parameters of chart production, are already interpreted expressions. But they do not present themselves as categories of interpretation, riven with ambiguity and uncertainty, because of the *representational* force of the visualization as a "picture" of "data." For instance, the assumption that gender is a binary category, stable across all cultural and national communities, is an assertion, an argument. Gendered identity defined in binary terms is not a self-evident fact, no matter how often Olympic committees come up against the need for a single rigid genital criterion on which to determine difference. By recognizing the always interpreted character of data we have shifted from data to capta, acknowledging the constructedness of the categories according to the uses and expectations for which they are put. Nations, genders, populations, and time spans are not self-evident, stable entities that exist a priori. They are each subject to qualifications and reservations that bear directly on and arise from the reality of lived experience. The presentation of the comparison in the original formulation grotesquely distorts the complexity, but also the basic ambiguity, of the phenomenon under investigation (nations, genders, populations). If the challenges we are facing were merely to accommodate higher levels of complexity into a data representation model, that would require one set of considerations and modifications. But the more profound challenge we face is to accept the ambiguity of knowledge, the fundamentally interpreted condition on which data is constructed, in other words, the realization of my refrain *that all data is capta.*

Humanistic methods

The humanistic aspect of this approach should be obvious: that knowledge created with the acknowledgment of the constructed nature of its premises is not commensurate with principles of certainty guiding empirical or realist methods. Humanistic methods are counter to the idea of reliably repeatable experiments or standard metrics that assume observer-independent phenomena. By definition, a humanistic approach is centered in the experiential, subjective conditions of interpretation. Phenomena and their observers are co-dependent, not necessarily in equal measure. A viewer gazing on a sublime landscape or recording migrations at a large scale may be more affected by the phenomena than the phenomena are by the observation. Theoretical physicist Werner Heisenberg never suggested that the relation of intervening observer and effect on phenomena was symmetrical, merely that it was codependent, when he introduced the concept of uncertainty in the early twentieth century.

Creating bar charts with ambiguity and degrees of uncertainty or other variables in them might cause champions of legibility and transparency some unease, but the shift away from standard metrics to metrics that express interpretation is an essential move for humanists and/or constructivists across disciplines. To emphasize the expressive quality of interpretation, I am going to characterize all information as *constructed*: as expressing the marks of its inflection in some formal way. The shift to expressive metrics and graphics is essential in changing from the *expression of constructed, interpretative information* to the *constructed expression of perceived phenomena*, but constructedness and inflection are not the only features of interpretative approaches. Capta is not an expression of idiosyncracy, emotion, or individual quirks, but a systematic expression of information understood as constructed, as phenomena perceived according to principles of observer-dependent interpretation. To do this, we need to conceive of every metric "as a factor of X," where X is a point of view, agenda, assumption, presumption, or simply a convention. By qualifying any metric as a factor of some condition, the character of the "information" shifts from self-evident "fact" to constructed interpretation motivated by a human agenda.[202]

The standard elements of graphic display for statistical information are simple and limited: scale divisions, coordinate lines, scale figures, circles, rectangles, curves, bars (or columns or percentages of pie charts or other forms) and labels (numbers and terms), signs of movement, flow, or state change (arrows, vectors, paths). The ordering and arrangement of elements within a chart create another level of information, relational information. Relational information is graphically produced; the ordering of elements by size, by color, by alphabetical order, by texture, shape, or other feature happens in graphical space. The resulting arrangement has a semantic value produced by features of proximity, grouping, orientation, apparent movement, and other graphical effects.

Now take these basic elements of graphical display and rethink them according to humanistic principles:

In conventional statistical graphics, the scale divisions are equal units. In humanistic, interpretative graphics, they are not.

In statistical graphics the coordinate lines are always continuous and straight. In humanistic, interpretative graphics, they might have breaks, repetitions, and curves or dips. Interpretation is stochastic and probabilistic, not mechanistic, and its uncertainties require the same mathematical and computational models as other complex systems.

The scale figures and labels in statistical graphics need to be clear and legible in all cases, and all the more so in humanistic, interpretative graphics since they will need to do quite a bit of work.

Perhaps the most striking feature distinguishing humanistic, interpretative, and constructivist graphical expressions from realist statistical graphics is that the curves, bars, columns, percentage values would not always be represented as discrete bounded entities, but as conditional expressions of interpretative parameters—a kind of visual fuzzy logic or graphical complexity. Thus their edges might be permeable, lines dotted and broken, dots and points might vary in size and scale or degree of ambiguity of placement. These graphical strategies express interpreted knowledge, situated and partial, rather than complete. They can be employed as systematically as other charting elements, though part of my intention is to disturb the grounds of certainty on which conventions of statistical legibility are based. Point of view systems introduced into graphs and charts will make evident a perspectival position with respect to their information, an inner standing point in the graphical rendering of space. This is true of all cartographic projections. Every map contains within its coordinate system for graphical expression a set of assumptions about the place from which the map is drawn. Information spaces drawn from a point of view, rather than as if they were observer-independent, reinsert the subjective standpoint of their creation into the graphical expression. Finally, any point or mark used as a specific node in a humanistic graph is assumed to have many dimensions to it, each of which complicates its identity by suggesting the embeddedness of its existence in a system of co-dependent relations. Information entities, or units, are thus understood as fictional abstractions serving a purpose. But their potential to be read again in relation to any number of other equally significant relations can be made evident. This approach destroys the ground on which standard metrics are used to abstract quantitative information from human circumstances. Humanistic premises replace notions of statistical concepts of self-identity with entangled co-dependence and contingencies.

All of this may sound unduly complicated to someone merely wanting to count the number of pupils enrolled in a group, calculate the number of pencils needed, or to show budgetary expenditures on a per capita basis in the classroom, for example. But this example—an instance of administrative and bureaucratic management—shows that such crudely conceived numeric statistics are useful only in the most reductive circumstances. They tell us nothing about whether the pencils can be used, whether the pupils are prepared or disposed to do their work, whether the budgets will have any effect on learning outcomes, or any of the other factors that come into play in assessments based on metrics extracted from lived experience. They do not account for the ecological, social, cultural, ideological, expertiential aspects of the larger system of which they are a part. But each metric—number of x or y—is actually a number as a factor of a particular intellectual assumption or decision: pupils as a factor of seats in a room, birthdates, population, illness; pencils as a factor of resource allocation, and so on. All metrics are metrics about something for some purpose.

The challenge is to design graphical expressions suited to the display of interpreted phenomena: information *about subjective user-dependent metrics, constructed displays of information*, and *inflected methods of graphical expression*. Interpretative construction registers point of view, position, the place from which and agenda according to which parameterization occurs. Constructedness does not align with the first term in a subjective/objective opposition. It is not individual inflection of mere idiosyncracy. Constructedness stresses co-dependent relations of observer and phenomena (in contrast to presumptions of objectivity, of observer-independent phenomena).

The display of information about affect often uses standard metrics. For example, a chart that shows mood changes or degrees of attraction or any other information related to subjectivity can be created with standard metrics and visual conventions.

The next task is more complicated. Constructed information (which is, in essence, all information, though for practical purposes, I insist on these approaches only in domains where the humanistic component of the interpretative act needs to be structured into the visualization), that is information whose constitution exhibits its situated, system-dependent character, deviates from the standard norms by using graphic variables such as intensity of tone, size, color, or other feature to embody its qualities. Constructed information can use graphical means to show its inflected character, demonstrating its deviation from standard norms in the way the display looks, or, in dynamic displays, *the way it acts*. One might imagine skittish points on an unstable grid to display the degrees of anxiety around a particular event or task, for instance, or points that glow hot or cold depending on the other elements that approach them. That would be *a constructivist display of information*.

Creating a display that uses *constructivist methods* of graphical expression extends this last example to the design of the basic visual structure. A constructivist grid used to show anxiety might have a widely varying set of spacings to show that the information on display is constituted as a variable of some other aspect of experience (number of family

members present at an event, for instance). Recognizing that
such methods are anathema to the empirically minded
makes even more clear that they are essential for the generation of graphical displays of interpretative and interpreted
information. The point is to create visualizations that expose,
rather than conceal, these principles of knowledge in the domains where the authority of information makes (still persistent and often pernicious) claims to "truth" through the
"transparency" of the visualization.

Visualizing interpretation

In proposing a new model for humanities' work, I am
suggesting that the subjective display of humanistic phenomena can be applied across the domains with which we are
concerned at four basic levels of interpretation or knowledge
production:

1) Modeling phenomenological experience in the making of humanities (*data* as *capta*, primary modeling, the representation of temporal and spatial experience);

2) Modeling relations among humanities documents,
i.e., discourse fields (a different metric might be needed to
understand dates on diplomatic documents from the spring
of 1944 or 1950);

3) Modeling the representations of temporality and spatiality that are found in humanities documents (narrative is
the most obvious);

4) Modeling the interpretation of any of the above
(depicting or graphing the performative quality of interpretation).[203]

The humanistic concept of knowledge depends upon
the interplay between a situated and circumstantial viewer

and the objects or experiences under examination and interpretation. That is the basic definition of humanistic knowledge, and its graphical display must be specific to this definition in its very foundational principles. The challenge is enormous, but essential, if the humanistic worldview, grounded in the recognition of the interpretative nature of knowledge, is to be part of the graphical expressions that come into play in the digital environment. If we do not engage with this challenge, we give the game away in advance, ceding the territory of interpretation to the ruling authority of certainty established on the false claims of observer-independent objectivity in the "visual display of quantitative information."[204]

I will conclude with one more concrete example of the shift from observer-independent realism to co-dependent constructivism. Snow's justly famous chart of deaths from cholera allowed city officials to track the source of the epidemic to a single water pump. The distribution of dots on the street map makes evident the role of the pump by the way they cluster. A useful map, crucial to analysis, its clarity and succinctness served an important purpose. It was sufficient to that purpose, adequate, but we could revisit that map and use it to express other factors. Who are those dots? Each individual has a profile, age, size, health, economic potential, family and social role. In short, each dot represents a life, and no life is identical. Many demographic features could be layered into this map to create a more complex statistical view of the epidemic. That is neither subjective data nor a subjective display. But what if we take the rate of deaths, their frequency, and chart that on a temporal axis inflected by increasing panic. Then give a graphical expression to the shape of the terrain, that urban streetscape, as it is redrawn to express the emotional landscape. Then imagine drawing this same streetscape from the point of view of a mother of six young children, a recent widow, a small child, or an elderly man whose son has just died. These latter are all instances of the graphical expression of humanistic interpretation. They are as different from the visual display of quantitative information as a close reading of a poem is from the chart of an eyetracker following movements across a printed page. They are fundamentally different in character and in their basic assumptions about the role of graphical expression as an aspect of knowledge production. We have a very long way to go in creating graphical expressions that serve humanistic interpretation, but I hope I have suggested some of the premises on which this work might begin.

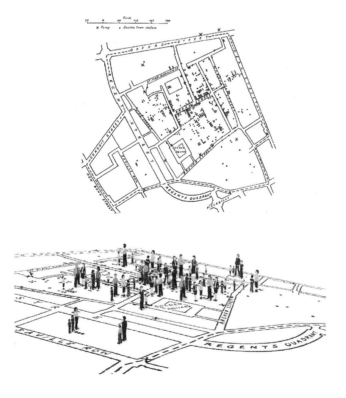

Snow original followed by point of view system built into the representation.

Interface and Interpretation

We tend to think of graphical interface
as the screen display, a portal into the
online world with menu bars, buttons,
and icons to manipulate. As a result,
we ignore its graphicality, its constructedness, the very features that support its
operations and make it work.
We look at interface as a thing, a representation of computational processes
that make it convenient for us to interact
with what is "really" happening.
But the interface is a mediating structure that supports behaviors and tasks.
It is a space between human users

and procedures that happen according to complicated protocols. But it also disciplines, constrains, and determines what
can be done in any digital environment.

Because engineering sensibilities have so dominated human-computer interaction, few attempts at humanistic approaches to design have come into play. Not only are there
sparse precedents for humanistic interface, but the very principles on which its design might proceed are not clearly outlined. The one place we can look for substantive precedents is
the long history of writing in humanistic traditions. Describing a codex book as an interface is glib if taken too literally.
But just as the graphical user interface should not be thought
of as a thing—reified, fixed, and stable—but as a mediating
apparatus, so the graphical features of the book should be understood as a spatially distributed set of graphical codes that
provide instructions for reading, navigation, access, and use.
Creating a continuum between electronic and print formats
and their features provides another useful synthesis of historical materials and future project design. A brief look at the history of interface design, interface theory, challenges for humanistic approaches to design, and the lessons to be taken
from bibliographical study will put a foundation in place. On
this basis we may move back and forth between a notion of
mise en page as design of composition, format features, graphical elements in electronic and print media, and a notion of
mise en scene or *mise en système*—an environment for action.

History of interface

We can gesture toward all sorts of historical examples:
switches and punch-cards, keyboards and all the many han-
dles, knobs, and inputs by which we interact with objects in

the world, or remediate communication into code. But in actuality, interface is a concept to which we have only paid attention for about fifty years. The term comes into play early in the process of computational design. The pioneering work of flight simulators, of head gear and foot pedals, and other apparatuses that would discipline the body to conform to a regime of screen-based and device-driven affordances made the discussion of relationships of human to machine into a field known as HCI.[205] These cockpit simulators involved the notion of distributed cognition, the realization that many aspects of embodied sensory and motor activity contribute to experience and knowledge.[206] Morton Helig's 1962 *Sensorama* bicycle and Myron Krueger's 1960s experiments with light-and-media ("Glowflow" and "Metaplay" experiments, and his essay "Video Place and Responsive Environment")

both emphasized the role of the body as an interface in ways that virtual reality pioneer Jaron Lanier picked up on in his designs meant to trick the entire sensorium into an illusion.[207]

In the late 1960s, when the only computer interface available was the text-based command line, Douglas Engelbart designed a prototype mouse about the same time as his contemporary, Ivan Sutherland, was creating Sketchpad, the first attempt at a real-time drawing program.[208] In 1970, Sutherland created a crude head-mounted display as one of several experiments with virtual reality devices. These pioneers realized that no matter how powerful computers were, they would not get used unless human beings could have a more direct connection with them than through the tedious

Microsoft
Flight Simulator
interface (2004).

communication of punch cards and switch settings. Engelbart and Sutherland were both engineers, tinkerers, whose approach to design combined imaginative innovation and the values of efficiency. The field of HCI gravitated toward engineers, not artists, and quickly became task-oriented, focused on feedback loops that minimized frustration and maximized satisfaction with mouse clicks and joy sticks and rewarding bells and whistles. In the 1970s, researchers at Xerox Parc, including Alan Kay, created a set of graphical icons grounded in the work of constructivist-oriented psychologists Jean Piaget and Jerome Bruner, who understood the constitutive and generative aspects of interface, not just the mechanistic features.[209] Visual conventions quickly established the language of interface iconography, first as a vocabulary of recognizable pictures of things, then as cues for their behavior and use.

Ivan Sutherland, Sketchpad (1963).

Star interface with desktop icons later copied and made ubiquitous.

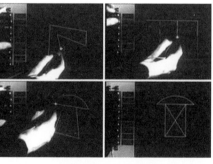

Professional interface designers chunk tasks and behaviors into carefully defined segments and "decision trees" to abstract their use from any hint of ambiguity. They analyze "user needs" into "functional requirements" in which concepts of "prototype," "user feedback," and "design" are locked into iterative cycles of "task specification" and "deliverables."[210] This language does not come from a theory of interface, but from

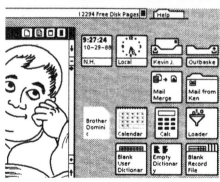

a platform of principles in the software industry. Deliberately mechanistic, it promotes the idea of a "user" instead of that of a humanistic "subject." Ben Shneiderman, whose justly renowned lab at the University of Maryland has been responsible for many trend-setting innovations, created "Eight Golden Rules" for interface design.[211] These were based on experiments testing short-term memory, capacity to follow cues from one screen to another, and so on. Common sense rules like "permit easy reversal of actions," have come to guide interface design as a result. Shneiderman's "user" is mainly a consumer, one who needs to be satisfied and kept engaged. His approach is grounded in the engineering, problem-solving pragmatism characteristic of the HCI community.

From these innovative beginnings came a robust industry that brought mass-market devices into production that were dominated by either Windows or Desktop metaphors.[212] The world divided into those who wanted to look *through* and those who wanted to look *at* their displays. More sophisticated object-oriented programming allowed icons to mimic behaviors of things they resembled so that a file folder could actually "open" on screen. The virtual performance was analogous to the physical one.

In addition to making use of different metaphors, interface design has followed several dominant models or ways of organizing communication with a user. An interface can express content, by presenting the intellectual structure of the site, repository, edition, or project for which it serves as portal (images, maps, texts, etc.). Or it can provide a set of instructions for actions and behaviors in the site by offering labels for tasks (search, browse, enter, view, login, contact us, etc.). Jesse James Garrett condensed the contrast between these two into a much cited graphic.[213] Garrett summarizes this fundamental duality between the web as an information space and as a task-supporting environment. His observation that the difference between these conceptions leads to confusion in design has implications for interface design in the basic tension between a rational organization of content and the need to balance this with an intuitive way of using that content. Interface is the space between these two—it is neither the transparent and self-evident map of content elements and their relations, nor is it simply a way to organize tasks. The two are as intimately related as the reading of a text in a book is governed by its graphical organization and the specific individual reading experience produced as a "performance" of that environment. [See Window 7, interface design]

A full theory of interface goes beyond the design of information structures and tasks into the realization that these are only the armature—not the essence—of that space of provocation in which the performative event takes place. And yet, we know that the structure of an interface *is* information, not merely a means of access to it. The search and the query modes are what I see. Sliders, for instance, with their implication of a smooth continuum, impose a model of what information is through their expression of how to manipulate a value, while a dialogue box that asks for a keyboarded number imposes an equally rigid model of discrete values. When we are looking for dates for travel, it will make an enormous difference whether we are able to state our request in discrete or continuous terms. Interface designers are fully versed in the strategic variables according to which information needs to be structured to be manipulated effectively.

Interface design has to take cultural differences into account. Pioneering work by Aaron Marcus and Associates studied web pages and their relation to various cultural factors.[214] Building on work by sociologist Geert Hofstede, they looked at the ways cultural value systems are expressed in

143

The concept of "high power distance" defined by Aaron Marcus and Geert Hofstede, *Cultural Dimensions and Global Web Design* (2001).

"Low power distance" defined by Marcus and Hofstede in *Cultural Dimensions and Global Web Design* (2001).

web design. Hofstede's categories, whatever quibbles they provoke, provided a way to look at design features across cultural categories such as different degrees of tolerance for ambiguity and uncertainty, greater value placed on individualism or a preference for collectivism, or different degrees of dissatisfaction with inequalities in power relations. Marcus and his associates showed that these features find expression in the graphic organization of information. Interactions with interface would, presumably, exhibit some similar features, though Marcus's group did not look at movement through the information structures or at the web architecture to see if that held true. If we look at web-based design, however, the navigation paths, search and query results, browse features—in brief, every aspect of the web content management and display—embody values, even if these are largely ignored or treated as transparent or invisible.

For the HCI community, the notion of a continuum of experience, within and structured by engagement with the interface, is never broken by engagement with representational content. So long as we think of interface as an environment for doing things, performing tasks, work, structuring behaviors, we remain linked to an idea that "reading" the digital environment is restricted to an analysis of its capacity to support the doing of tasks. This suggests that interface work is happening on what we would call a plane of discourse, or the level of the telling, rather than the told. The notion of HCI is that the single "frame" is that of the user experience. Thus a mantra like Shneiderman's "Overview first, zoom and filter, details on demand" assumes that one is working in a very restricted, highly structured, bounded, and discrete environment.[215] For interactive database design, his approach makes sense, since there the interface is a way of displaying search results that come from the combination of variables or filters. Dynamic information visualization flattens the planes of reference, discourse, and processing so that they appear to be a single self-evident surface. The naivete of that approach is easily critiqued: it is semiotic child's play to take a graphical interface with sliders, windows, dials, and variables and demonstrate that it is an expression of motivations, agendas, and deliberately concealed factors, no matter how earnestly or usefully it may serve a specific purpose. This is true whether we turn our critical attention on Travelocity, Yahoo, Flickr, or Lifelines2 and its display of "temporal categorical patterns across multiple records."

The human factors and HCI communities work to design effective environments, ones in which satisfactions are balanced with frustrations, and efficiency can be maximized. Their focus is on the literal structure of the design, the placement of buttons, amount

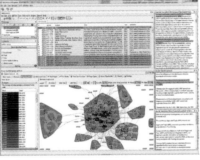

Action Science Explorer, complex data integration interface.

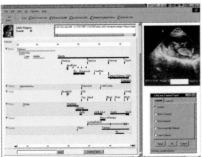

Lifelines interface, timeline created from experiential data.

of time it takes to perform a task, how we move through screens, and so on. In "The Theory Behind Visual Interface Design," Mauro Manelli lays out a comprehensive mechanistic approach to the stages of action involved from "forming an intention" and "specifying an action" to "evaluating the outcome."[216] Manelli's approach reflects on the design process in relation to a concept of "user experience" that approaches to map structure and effect directly. This is akin to doing close readings of a text's formal features as if it locked that text into the reading. We need to theorize interface and its relation to reading as an environment in which varied behaviors of embodied and situated persons will be enabled differently according to its many affordances. This shifts us away from the HCI world, and the interface, into fields closer to graphic design and media theory, an important move in reading and designing interface.

Considerable distance separates the interface design community and that concerned with critical theory. Interface theory has to close that gap.

Interface theory

From a humanist perspective, our understanding of digital interface should build on critical study of the subject in literary, media, and visual studies. We need a theory of the ways interface produces subjects of enunciation, not users as consumers. The HCI "user" combines two ideological illusions in a single paradoxical identity: the predictability of a mechanized automaton and the myth of autonomous agency. Humanistic approaches to interface need to recuperate the theoretical formulation of subjectivity as a part of the enunciative apparatus, of positions spoken, articulated, created by the structuring and desiring machines of representations. The legacy of a half century or more of theoretical discourse is available for this work, ready to be brought back into play. Who is the subject of an interface? How are we produced as subjects of the discourses on the screen? And in our embodied and culturally situated relations to screens and displays? These are fundamental questions that precede the analysis of content models or knowledge design, questions addressed to the very situation in which such models are located and used as instruments, consciously or not, of institutionalized relations of power. This is familiar language, the recognizable critical discussion of ideological formations as they work through individual subjects through the codes and features of mediated representations—language, image, ritual, spatial relations, and other cultural systems.

In 1989, Norman Long, a sociologist, described interface as "a critical point of interaction between life worlds."[217] Twenty years ago, Brenda Laurel defined interface as a surface where the necessary contact between interactors and tasks allowed functions to be performed.[218] She noted that these were sites of power and control, infusing her theoretical insight with a critical edge lacking from the engineering sensibility of most of the HCI community. Interface is a dynamic space in a psychoanalytic sense, not just a psychological one. Like any other component of computational systems, it is an artifact of complex processes and protocols, a zone in which our behaviors and actions take place, but it is also a symbolic space in which we constitute ourselves through the experience of its particular structures and features. Interface *is what we read* and *how we read* combined through engagement, it is a provocation to cognitive experience, but it is also an enunciative apparatus.

"Task optimization" is a watchword in the interface

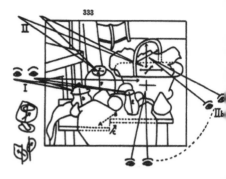

Erle Loran,
diagram showing
point of view
systems structured
into a Cezanne
painting, *Cezanne's
Composition*
(1943).

Lisa Snyder,
Perspective
rendering of
virtual
reconstruction
of Columbian
Exposition of 1893.

community, largely as a result of Jakob Nielson's work on web usability in which interface mediates between information structures and user needs.[219] But the "enunciated subjects" of interface mentioned above have had little critical play by contrast, and the humanistic agenda can go a step further. A humanistic subject leaves a trace on the emerging, mutating environment of an interface. The crucial definition of human subjectivity is that it can register a trace of itself in a representational system, and that self-recognition and self-constitution depend on that trace, that capacity to make and register difference. The encounter between a subject and an interface need not be understood mechanistically. We can think beyond representational models to understand interface as an ecology, a border zone between cultural systems and human subjects.

Rather than being user-centered, a humanistic design approach is subject-oriented. Such an approach would not just include accommodation to whim, preference, habits of thought, customs of taste, and differences of reading. After all, even the most empirical clinical studies show that we don't read mechanistically. Eye tracking experiments support the "production" of an interface and its "producing" effect on a reader/viewer as surely as any theoretical deconstruction of reading as information transfer.[220] An interface launches a probabilistic missive in the direction of a user/reader, but the reading is always an act of self-production and of textual deformation. But subject-oriented interface includes recognition that a point of view system is in place, that a subject enunciates, produces, a constitutive perspective in which she is situated, made, and from which she perceives. Point of view structures the world and positions us in its representations. All images have a point of view. They are all drawn from some place in relation to what is shown. Perspectival systems position a stationary viewer whose cone of vision is transected by a plane.[221] Orthographic systems assume a viewer positioned at equal distances from each bit of the observed object, an unrealizable fiction, but a useful one. The screen space—and subdivided spaces within it—each assume a relation to the viewing subject whose gaze is expected to produce an experience of the world within its frames.

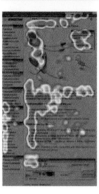

So prevalent have notions of interface become that cognitive scientist Donald Hoffman has taken them as the founding image of his "Interface Theory of Perception."[222] He argues against representational models of perception, stating that animals do not represent the world to themselves in a truthful or veridical way, but through what he terms "icon models." Our relation to our environment is adaptive, mediating through the abstraction of an interface that supports "sufficing" behaviors. The icon models organize our behaviors rather than representing the world. A good example is the model of "real time" that we project onto computer interfaces and their refresh rate. Nothing about that metric is "real," except that it describes the limit of our perception of temporal units, the point at which we cannot perceive delay. But because the metaphors of screen environments are so

Nielsen Norman Group, eye tracking results, "F-Shaped Pattern for Reading Web Content" (2006).

familiar, we do not see them as models, but simply cues for actions. Similarly, we take little notice of the way screen spaces already address us, speak us by organizing the discourse of their display according to expectations of who is using a particular interface. As surely as point of view systems in visual works embody the subject whose position organizes the work around their gaze, so interfaces are constitutive environments that model experience through experience. And as in any enunciative system, our subjectivity is as much an effect of what we cannot say, what cannot be done, the constraints on behavior and imagination, as of what we do and can perform directly. The old spectre of "disciplinary regimes" that order relations of power rises immediately into view in taking the measure of interface design.[223]

Gestalt principles can certainly be used to read a graphical user interface.[224] But we should also make use of the terms of theatricality and identification laid out by media theorists in their analyses of the ways viewers are absorbed into the flow of digital and online environments.[225] For decades, these theoretical formulations have taken into account the structures of the gaze, the identification with the situation of viewing, the production of subject positions in relation to the act of engagement with media as well as the con-

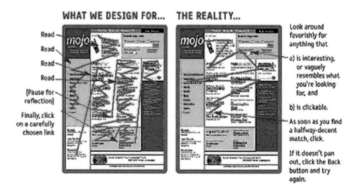

Steve Krug, from *Don't Make Me Think* (2005).

tent of representation. Fundamental questions arise about who speaks and who is spoken. The place from which a discourse is produced is often erased. In whose interest is it to efface the origin of a discourse so that it naturalizes the production of information on the screen? The display simply appears to be "there" and we "simply" seem to absorb it. We pick and choose from a menu whose design we do not question because it seems neutral. These positions begin to chip away at the premises on which actor-network theory works, since it assumes the discrete autonomy of the actor/agent distinct from the network. That very concept is mechanistic, and at odds with the integrative co-dependencies that are essential to a critical humanistic understanding of interface. Instead of a boundary, or "between" space, an interface becomes a codependent in-betweenness in which speaker and spoken are created. The idea of a performative interface follows immediately from this, and serves well to expand a humanistic approach.

The standard theory of interface, based on the "user experience," is reductively mechanistic. Its goal is to design an environment to maximize efficient accomplishment of tasks —whether these are instrumental, analytic, or research oriented—by individuals who are imagined as autonomous agents whose behaviors can be constrained in a mechanical feedback loop. Challenges to that conception arise from within the information studies community—where interface is embedded in the motivations of an embodied user engaged in some activity that may or may not be goal oriented, highly structured, and/or driven by an outcome—but might equally be the diversionary experience of wandering, browsing, meandering, or prolonging engagement for the purpose of pleasure or an even lower level notion like keeping boredom at bay or idle distraction and time squandering. This aesthetic paradigm has had its advocates such as aesthetic theorist Roy Ascott, artists like those who comprise jodi.org, or new media artists like Casey Reas, Scott Sona Snibbe, or the host of others whose work populates analog and digital gallery and exhibit spaces.[226] In their work, aesthetic dimensions and imaginative vision make interface a space of being and dwelling, not a realm of control panels and instruments only existing to be put at the service of something else. The jodi projects were often disruptive, disorienting, frustrating in their defeat of expectations—and thus their undoing of conventions of user and task. Snibbe's work engages users through interaction and remediation, taking data into graphic form so it can be manipulated, played with, and thus take the viewer by surprise.

I bring up these contrasting communities because they challenge the illusion of interface as a *thing*, immediately making it clear that a theory of interface cannot be constructed around expectations of performance, tasks, or behaviors.

Reading interface

Web environments are more mutable and modular than films, and the analogy between old media and new breaks down when we realize that all segments of film, no matter how radically they are spliced and combined, are segments of the same order of thing.[227] They may, and do, require significant jumps in cognitive framing, but they are part of the same modality: film texts/sequences. All film segments and video segments unfold according to the same set of temporal principles: continuous and forward moving in a unidirectional manner. But the temporalities of web environments are varied. They don't conform to a single mode. The refresh

rate of headlines, stories, videos, ads, banners, pop-ups, stories, other reports, links, and user contributed information
are all different. But also, the ways our bodies engage with
these are distinct at the level of manipulation and cognitive
processing of the experience.

If I watch an embedded video, track events on a map
that zooms, scales, and shifts between a schematic map to a
street view with its photographic codes while I am reading
through a text, following links, opening a series of windows,
and so on, then what is it that constitutes the interface? And
what organizes the relational experience? Unlike the controlled experience of viewing a film, reading a graphic novel,
or even performing the discontinuous reading of a book or
newspaper, this experience has no a priori unifying ground
on which the fragments relate. The exterior frame of a graphic novel, the defining frame that delimits its boundaries, has
more porousness and more fragility in a web environment.
We note the limits of a site or repository, which may have the
isolation and autonomy of a silo. But in most web environments, we are reading across a multiplicity of worlds, phe-

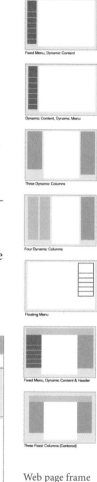

Web page frame
conventions.

TheAtlantic.com
frame structure.

nomena, representations, arguments, presentations, and media modalities. The way we make connections across these disparities is different than when we work in a single delimited frame. The points of connection are perhaps best described in terms of mathematical figures and architectural spaces: as nodes, edges, tangents, trajectories, hinges, bends, pipelines, portals. These are not the language of old media transferred to new, not a language that derives from theories of montage or cuts, editing or pastiche, allegory or appropriation. Instead, these are structuring principles that refer to the constitutive nature of interface experiences of reading.

Reading was always a performance of a text or work, always an active remaking through an instantiation. But reading rarely had to grapple with the distinctions between immersion and omniscience—as when we are experiencing the first person view of a video juxtaposed with manipulation of a scalable map, with watching the social network reconfigure itself around a node of discourse even as the node is changing. Digital environments increasingly depend upon a whole series of contingent texts, transient documents, that are created on the fly by search and query, filtered browsing, or other results-based displays that last only a few moments on the screen in the stepping-stone sequence of user clicks that move from one ephemeral configuration to the next. In addition, the scale issues of reading across large corpora have produced numerous data mining approaches for distant reading, a term made popular by Franco Moretti. Like Lev Manovich's cultural analytics, the approach depends on analysis of information in the digital files to present patterns of theme, sentiment, or other values at a scale impossible for human readers. Such projects often contain more hours of audio, visual, textual, or video files than could be looked at by a single individual across the span of a lifetime. Reading is thus augmented by computational capacities, though the questions of meaning and value, and of the specific identity of those digitally produced surrogates and syntheses, pose new questions about the nature of reading and role of interface as provocation.

The dynamic nature of the interface environment reconfigures our relation to the act of reading, ratcheting up the insistence on a constructivist approach that understands perception as a constitutive act. Countering traditional notions of perception as a species' ability to "address the true properties of the world, classify its structure, and evolve our senses to this end," Hoffman suggests that perception is a "species-specific user interface that guides behavior." Like the Chilean biologists Francesco Varela and Humberto Maturana, he demonstrates that no experience exists a priori, the world and its reading come into being in a codependent relation of affordances.[228] The new affordances of web-based reading are not distinct from this, they are not another order of thing, a representation already made and structured, but a set of possibilities we encounter and from which we constitute the tissue of experience. The constitutive act, however, in this new environment puts our bodies—eyes, ears, hands, heads—and our sensory apparatus into relation with rapidly changing modes. The integration of these into a comprehensible experience seems to have emerged intuitively, since the frames within frames of the web interface provide sufficient cues to signal the necessary shifts of reading modes.

Erving Goffman's frame analysis is particularly relevant to the processing of a web environment where we are constantly confronted with the need to figure out what domain or type of information is being offered and what tasks, behaviors, or possibilities it offers.[229] To reiterate, on its own a typology of graphical elements does not account for the ways in which format features provoke meaning production in a reader or viewer. The cognitive processing that occurs in the relation between such cues and a viewer is not mechanistic, predictable, or linear, but probablistic. Graphical features organize a field of visual information, but the activity of reading follows other tendencies. These depend on embodied and situated knowledge, cultural conditions and training, the whole gamut of individually inflected and socially conditioned skills and attitudes. Frame analysis is a schematic outline that formalizes certain basic principles of ways we process information into cognitive value or go from stimulus to cognition. Filling in the details of ideological and hegemonic cues, or reading specific artifacts as a production of an encounter—the production of text (reading) and production of a subject of the text (reader)—is a process that depends on specific cases. But the generalized scheme of frame analysis puts in place a crucial piece of our model of interface: the recognition that any piece of perceived information has to be processed through a set of analytic frames that are grounded in cognitive experience *in advance* of being read as meaningful. We have to know where we are in the perceptual-cognitive loops—what scale the information is and what domain it belongs to, for instance—before we can make any sense of it at all.

In a networked environment, such as an iPhone for instance, the literal frames of buttons and icons form one set of organizing features. They chunk, isolate, segment, distinguish one activity or application from another, establishing the very basis of expectation for a user. Engagement follows, and then returns to the interface in an ongoing process of co-dependent involvement. But "frames" are not the same as these conspicuous graphical instances. Once we move away from the initial menu of options and into specific applications or digital environments, a user is plunged into the complex world of interlocking frames—commerce, entertainment, information, work, communication—whose distinction within the screen space and interface depend on other conventions. For scholarly work, the ultimate focus of my inquiry, the relation among frames is integral to the relations of what are traditionally considered text and paratext. In a digital environment, those relations are loosened from their condition of fixity and can be reorganized and rearranged according to shifting hierarchies of authority and priority. A footnote to one text becomes the link to a text which becomes the primary text in the next window or frame, and so forth.

The basic tenets of frame analysis depend on a vocabulary for describing relations (rather than entities). Frames by definition depend on their place within a cognitive process of decision making that is sorting information along semantic and syntactic axes, reading the metaphoric value of images and icon as well as their connection to larger wholes of which they are a part. In traditional frame theory certain behaviors are attributed to relations between frames. A frame can extend, intensify, connect, embed, juxtapose, or otherwise modify another frame and perception. The terminology is spatial and dynamic. It describes cognitive processes, not simple actions of an autonomous user, but codependent relations of user and system. In invoking frame analysis as part of the diagrammatic model of interpretation, we have moved from a traditional discussion of graphical formats as elements of a *mise en page* to a sense that we are involved with a *mise en scene* or *système*. This puts us on the threshold of interface and a theory of constructivist processes that constitute the interface as a site of such cognitive relations. Interface is not a thing, but a zone of affordances organized to support and provoke activities and behaviors probabilistically, rather than mechanically. Only by taking into full account the constructivist process of codependence that is implicit in frame analysis have we been able to move from a simple description of graphic features—as if they automatically produce certain effects—to a realization that the graphical organization only provides the provocations to cognition. They constrain and order the possibilities of meaning producing conditions, but do not produce any effect automatically. In fact, the very term "user" needs to be jettisoned—since it implies an autonomy and agency independent of the circumstances of cognition—in favor of the "subject" familiar from critical theory. Interface theory has to proceed from the recognition that it is an extension of the theory of the subject, and that therefore the engineering approach to interface that is so central to HCI practitioners will need some modification.

Humanistic interface

Before we launch into speculation, however, and offer a vision for reconfiguring arguments into constellationary form using the techniques of semantic web, topic maps, network diagrams, and other computational means of visualization and spatializing relations among units of thought, we should pause to examine a few striking instances of interface design that incorporate humanistic principles in their organization. One way this is accomplished is for an interface to express a content model that comes from critical study, editing, bibliography, or other traditions rooted in the appreciation and engagement with cultural materials. The Van Gogh Correspondence project is exemplary in this regard, offering a view into the repository that is structured by categories that emerge from the material.[230] Correspondents have senders and receivers, they have places from which they originate and to which they are sent. Van Gogh's letters contain images, sketches, which are often related to paintings or other works, larger projects, and their development. The site features the facsimiles of the letters and their transcriptions in versions that respect their lineation as well as translate them into multiple languages for broader access and use. The fundamental considerations structuring the interface arose from the belief that these aesthetic materials would be studied, used, and analyzed, not consumed. The Austrian Academy's *Die Fackel* archive, a completely transcribed, marked-up, analysis of the work of the cultural critic Karl Kraus allows for faceted search and browsing of the entire run of the journal from 1899 to 1936.[231] The design of the interface, created by Anne Burdick, uses subtle choices in color palette, typography, and graphical features to push the substantive content of facsimiles, search results, and transcription/analysis into the foreground. The complex navigation and orientation features that guide a reader and show where he or she is at any moment relative to the archive as a whole produce a structuring effect that is situated within recognizable frames. At every point we know where we are, how we arrived, and how to move around while making use of the analytic features built into the project. If the Van Gogh project expresses a model of humanistic content, the *Die Fackel*

Interface design for the Vincent Van Gogh Letters Project.

Anne Burdick Design, *Die Fackel* web site design.

Greg Crane, interface for the Perseus Digital Library.

Interface for the Encyclopedia of Chicago.

project creates a humanistic environment that supports question, analysis, and study.

Two other exemplary projects are Greg Crane's long-standing Perseus library of classical materials and the Chicago Encyclopedia.[232] These offer a very different user experience through their argument structure and knowledge design. They share certain features, in particular, a rich information infrastructure that cross-references terms, concepts, keywords, sources, citations, and indices. Each is designed to allow multiple kinds of use and pathways, views into the data and content, through analytic process as well as reading experiences. Neither has a single voice or narrative that organizes the whole into a linear presentation, though either may be used to read documents and interpretative materials in a linear way.

Each optimizes, sometimes minimally, the use of graphical organization for navigation and orientation. The distinctive features that ground these interfaces and sites in a humanistic inquiry is the combination of content models derived from humanities content and the conviction that individual reading and study make the experience anew in each instance. The interface supports production of reading, rather than consumption of experience.

Taking humanistic principles one step further, the artists Jonathan Harris and Sep Kamvar's project, *We Feel Fine*, registers participants' engagement by harvesting indicators of emotional states from publically available Twitter feeds, Facebook postings, and social media of all kinds.[233] The site is a pulse, an indicator, a living system in which collective emotional life is registered. The faceted search allows a viewer to select various criteria from demographic data banks and get a read on the state of mind of a defined segment of the population. Because the data is constantly refreshed and updated, the user can be part of the feedback loop that generates the next round of response. Obviously issues of scale play a part, and no individual user makes a statistically significant difference, but that the system is driven by the constant recalibration of expressions of emotional experience gives the project humanistic resonance. This dimension, of registering affective qualities of human experience, extends the mechanistic boundaries of computational processing into a dynamic relation with living beings whose continually differentiating experience is its lifeblood and core. As the force and shape of interpretation begins to register on the humanistic corpus that contributes to the many streams of cultural material, incorporating these processes of assessment and reflection has the potential to produce new ways of gauging and engaging with the affective experience of being human.

Christian Nold, biomapping, from *Emotional Cartography* (2009).

Lessons from bibliography

Not only is it interesting to think about the book as an interface, but we can build on those insights for understanding how interfaces actually work. As is the case of screen interfaces, we tend to see the features of a book page as things, rather than as cues for reading and use. The purpose of headers, footers, page numbers, margins, gutters, indentations, tables of contents, indices, and every other bit of text and paratext is to structure our reading. Solid blocks of undifferentiated text would be difficult to digest, even though this was the earlier condition from which the conventions of the codex as we know it have emerged.

All of the graphic features of the book have functions. They work as presentation (what's inscribed and present), representation (content of a text and/or image), navigation (wayfinding across the spaces of the book), orientation (sense of where one is in the whole), reference (into the sources and conversations on which a work is drawn), and social networking (the dialogues of commentary, footnotes, endnotes, and marginalia). Just like a web page, a book is a site of social exchange. Its apparent stability and fixity are an illusion. A book is a kind of snapshot across a stream of exchanges and debates, especially a scholarly book. The dynamic properties usually attributed to new media are already active and present within older forms.

But where, when, and how did this scholarly book apparatus emerge?

When the codex book form first appeared in the second and third centuries of the Common Era, the design of its page spaces drew on habits established with scrolls and tablets for the arrangement of text in lines and columns.[234] In these, as well as in manuscripts, we see many instances of graphical syntax that is semantically coded, such as basic reading order and direction. In the early centuries of the codex, its textual inscriptions lack almost all other scoring features. There were no spaces between words, no punctuation, no apparatus for searching or organizing a text, no call outs, no headers, no subheads, no tables of contents, no indices. Texts supported continuous reading, but not searching or discontinuous use.

Schematic organizations gradually emerged to distinguish what we would call content types, or different aspects of texts, sorted by their identities, as captions, chapter titles, notes, and the like took on distinct roles and graphical forms. In his struggle to establish the authority of biblical texts, the third century scholar Origen created structured graphic devices to organize his work.[235] A multi-columned table (*hexapla*) that resembled an editorial spreadsheet was used to compare variant texts. Other conventions, such Canon tables that make use of architectural motifs to create and reference structural divisions of space, served as mediating interfaces to

Codex Sinaiticus (mid-fourth century), British Library.

match passages and references in Gospel texts. Similar tabular structures were then used to order other kinds of information, such as the contents of almanacs or chronicles. The very act of ruling a vellum or parchment sheet creates a grid structure whose reasoned syntax may be put at the service of various knowledge representations.[236] Books are structured spaces as surely as web pages with their wireframe organization.

According to the medievalist Malcolm Parkes, the scholarly book as we know it assumed its familiar form between the twelfth and fifteenth centuries.[237] This was an era of cultural transformation with regard to knowledge and the technologies for its creation and dissemination. In the emerging intellectual centers of Spain, France, England, Italy, and Portugal, increasing professionalization, interest in secular knowledge and canon law, and changing conditions for urbanization gave rise to universities as self-regulating communities that were sanctioned either by civil or religious entities. The earlier, almost exclusive claim of monasteries to serve as the centers of knowledge production and preservation in the West began to dissolve after the twelfth century. The establishment of new mendicant orders, Dominicans, Franciscans, in the early thirteenth century created a need for new, different, scholarly resources. Itinerant preachers wanted a single, all-purpose book that could be carried and used extensively as a reference work—it was also all they could afford. Their needs in part restructured the format of the scholarly book.

In "The Influence of *Ordinatio* and *Compilatio* on the

Canon tables,
Book of Kells
(circa 800).

Development of the Book," Parkes writes: "The late medieval book differs more from its early medieval predecessors than it does from the printed books of our own day. The scholarly apparatus that we take for granted—analytical table of contents, text disposed into books, chapters, and paragraphs, and accompanied by footnotes and index—originated in the applications of notions of *ordinatio* and *compilatio* by writers, scribes, rubricators of the thirteenth, fourteenth, and fifteenth centuries."[238] In detailing the conditions under which these features come into being, Parkes traces changes in reading practice from a monastic *lectio* that was meditative and linear to a scholastic one that was active, non-linear, characterized by cross-referencing, synthesis, and argument. Thus the changes in "mise-en-page of texts were bound up with the developments in the methods of scholarship and changes in attitudes to study." Earlier codices used a format that had little textual apparatus surrounding it, because no perceived

Origen		THE NEW SCHAFF-HERZOG				270
Hebrew.	Hebrew Transliterated.	Aquila.	Symmachus.	LXX.	Theodotion.	Variants.

Hexapla for critical editing, *The New Schaff-Herzog Encyclopedia of Religious Knowledge* (1908-1914).

need existed. Elaborate commentaries and glosses made use of graphical means for distinguishing different orders of text. These visual distinctions also support navigation through a bound book, with call outs, headers, and other features assisting the practice of discontinuous reading. In addition to helping locate specific chapters or verses, these new paratexts made it possible to sustain a scholarly system of reliable citation. The advantages of graphical organization became readily apparent and were copied extensively as well as expanded.

Once the conventional features of page layout are understood as elements developed to serve functions, their design goes beyond harmonious layout or pleasing proportions. The page structures conventionalized in medieval manuscripts are adopted into printed books and digital documents. They permit clear encoding of the relations of text to commentary, text to paratext, and apparatus to the whole space of the book. In digital formats, some of these features

Decretals of Pope Gregory IX with the Gloss of Bernard of Parma (second half of thirteenth century).

are imitated without understanding the purpose that they served, and without understanding that orientation and navigation are features of the codex that have yet to be worked out systematically in digital documents. So conventionalized are the elements of texts and their codified relations that we author with those structures in mind. A table of contents, added at the end of a project as if it were the summary and introduction to the whole, is both a fiction and a highly formula-driven piece of writing. The text has to be produced in conformance with expectations, composed under graphical constraint. Footnotes point outward to the discourse field of textual production, to the communities with which an author is in dialogue. These find their way into sidebars and hyperlinks, even as other conventions have quickly arisen in the organization of screen space that guide its allocation to different purposes according to positions. Just as a running header on a page or a page number on the outside edge is a device whose presence arises from use, so equivalents in digital environments have been created on the basis of functionality, not just as graphical features. The aside, the comment, the marginal note, the index, and chapter heads or subheads, are part of our process of composition (and certainly employed in the processes of editing). They guide our writing in advance of reading. Or have. Things are changing. New writing modes are shaped by social media, by email, blogs, Twitter, and wikis. In these changing conventions the surface of interface often conceals the back-end technical and conceptual processes by which they are produced. Collaborative modes of writing, as in wiki production, absorb individual authors into texts at the word, phrase, and fragment level. Attribution and citation do not mark themselves on the front pages as a brand and introduction, but have to be sought in bylines or citation indices. Navigation and display are increasingly intertwined as well, with analytic processing and data mining generating on-the-fly visualizations that can be used as points of entry to search, retrieve, or engage with the files represented onscreen. The rules are more complicated, less obvious, less accessible, at least for the present. We rely on spatial specificity to organize written language (or multimedia texts, for that matter). As new functionalities begin to emerge in the modular and data driven organization of interconnected corpora, the features that have to be structured into designs for use are also changing. The tactile user interface supports scale changes, diving and drilling, expansion and compression, in ways that the material substrate of paper could only hint at.

The shift from manuscript page to layouts dependent on print technology reinforced tendencies toward squareness (quadrature) and invariant type size and style. These are not absolute requirements for printed pages, but production means—letterpress, linotype, phototype, and digital typesetting—were all designed to support these conventions. By contrast, for manuscript pages to contain lines of text that are evenly sized and spaced demands disciplined attention to the calligraphic tasks. The affordances of each medium are fundamentally different. The lower limits of micrographia are determined only by the ability of a scribe to manipulate the point of a pen, and insertion of one line after another into the space between two pre-existing lines of text is governed only by a principle of elasticity, not strict decorum. When we look at the elaborated commentaries that decorate the pages of manuscripts in the Middle Ages, when conventions of navigation, reading, and writing were being established as customs for use, we see the origins of our habits alongside the opportunities that had to be let go within the constraints of printed forms. Digital environments have imitated the

squareness of print, though in fact
no feature in the technology determines this, just conventions of
design and reading. Pad devices
have integrated the scale-chang-
ing capacities of digital display,
previously activated with zoom
icons or percentage values, into
the tactile interface. Conceptualizing conventions and roles for
spatial relations among semantic
elements in these modes goes far
beyond the fantasies of hypertext
that initially seemed to be the
horizon of opportunity for the
exploded or extended book.

A striking instance of con-
ventionalization appears in the rules governing the placement of interpretative texts in the published versions of commentary on the Torah, known as the Talmud.[239] The earliest
printed editions were created in Venice in the 1480s.[240] The
comprehensive commentaries of the late eleventh century
scholar, Rabbi Solomon ben Isaac (referred to by an acronym
based on his initials, Rashi), were placed in a regular position
as the four lines in the uppermost right hand corner of the
page.[241] This format was adopted by the sixteenth century
printer Daniel Bomberg for his layout of the Babylonian
Talmud. The design came into wide circulation in a format
that continues in use to the present day.[242] The Talmud's
graphical organization not only puts textual elements into a
design structure that carries semantic value, it also encodes
assumptions about the consensual system of knowledge production within a community. Reading practices are coded to

*Corpus Juris
Canonici*, vol. 2
(Rome 1582);
UCLA Special
Collections.

appeal to and signal a self-acknowledged and self-identifying group. The page serves as a specific site of mediation, a record of exchange within a tradition whose participants know and perpetuate its codes. They do not just know how to read the book, they know they are identified by its format as its implied readers. Similar observations could be brought to bear on other complex

texts whose commentary and scholarly apparatus serve specialized fields of knowledge—law, religious doctrine, philosophy, and so on across varied disciplines of human inquiry—where the space of the page holds the conversation in place, marking its dialogues and exchanges, debates and contentious struggles. Printed and manuscript pages are and were their own snapshot of a continuum of socially networked exchanges. Their flexibility and mutability has much to offer to the current investigation of design for humanistic work.

The enthusiasm for innovation that came with the first wave of hypertext writing in the 1980s brought equal parts insight and exaggeration to the idea of creating imaginative works that played with diagrammatic features.[243] Earlier visions of branching narratives are usually tracked to Vannevar Bush's 1945 paper, "As We May Think," to the first works published by Theodor Nelson in the 1960s, or in some of the experiments of innovative writers who played with alternative

Page from the Vilna edition of the Babylonian Talmud (circa 1880).

structures in analogue or digital work, such as Julio Cortazar in *Hopscotch*, first published in 1963, or the computationally generated text first published in 1984, *The Policeman's Beard Is Half-Constructed*.[244] Artists had made projects that used alternative physical and graphical structures—decks of cards, collage techniques, combinatoric processes—in analogue form since early Dada experiments in the 1910s.[245] But hyperbolic critical claims exaggerated the binaristic distinction between the linearity of print and the non-linearity of programs like Hypercard.[246] Designed for Apple and launched in 1987, Hypercard was a milestone, offering an easy to use platform for creating combinatoric works built in chunks whose sequence did not have to be locked into the single linear sequence. The possibilities seemed limitless. Branching and linking, the basic underpinnings of the web, were embodied in its programming. The structure of hypertext could be rendered in a diagram, as well as experienced as multiple pathways through the reading. Hypertext chunking allowed a conceptual separation between content types (such as footnotes, sources, citations, primary materials, and other elements) to be made more explicit in the storage, and thus manipulation, of these units. This modular quality served to break a text into narrative units for combinatoric play, with relations specified in links, or in a database structure.

Hypertext map from the early history of the World Wide Web (circa 1990).

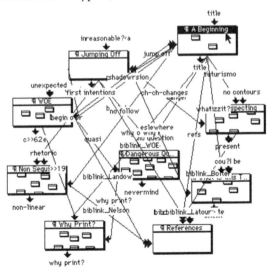

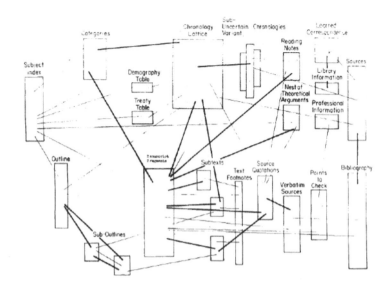

These ways of working have become so integral to our daily practice that we barely pause to consider their structuring principles or effects.

Now hypertext seems quaint, its tropes evoke nostalgia rather than future visions. Augmented displays and networked databases that produce real-time texts from protocols that are geo-spatially located, or triggered by data profiles and personae, or other automated processes, make hypertext seem like child's play in an early sandbox of digital imaginings. Nonetheless, our critical engagement with database rhetoric as a compositional mode lags behind. The notion of creating content types to undergird creative or even critical scholarly writing and shaping discourse production as an extension of data formats is only the province of a few experimental writers or scholars. Digital display and the behaviors afforded by APIs, application programming interfaces, have generated the aesthetic vocabulary that drives most new forms of textual production online. Back-end conceptu-

Ted Nelson, Xanadu file structure, devised in 1965, from "Back to the Future" (2007).

al thinking as a compositional method, with spatialized and graphical relations expressing semantic values, occurs only in rare or technical instances, usually performed by professionals in information fields or artists with programming skills. We have a way to go before a broader swath of the literate population has the compositional/computational skills to push beyond bibliographical conventions and into digitally driven design concepts.

The binarism stressed by early hypertext writers and theorists suggested that the compositional techniques that took up Jorge Luis Borges's image of the "garden of forking paths" heralded the arrival of a new era of literary liberation from the tedium of linearity imposed by conventions of print.[247] In pausing to think about the ways authoring absorbs and depends on provocations coded into the graphical space that maps relations among one bit of text and another, we are bringing questions about the authoring platforms and potential/*poetential* of electronic space into view. Formats in electronic space have reprised some of the older textual modes of production, even as these are interpenetrated with the now ubiquitous structure of cross references and linking. Blogs are scroll forms, social media sites are galleries, a list of tweets has diagrammatic codes, a Wiki divides its screen display into topic, introduction, and overview outline. Many of these formats do not mimic any particular script predecessor, even if they preserve footnotes, references, or citations organized according to print conventions. Scrolling texts, pop up windows, rapid refresh in screen displays, all introduce a more rapid temporal rate of re-inscription than print allowed, but the flat space of display to which most screen writing is reduced is, if anything, far less graphically sophisticated than the spatialized physicality of a three-dimensional codex. When we consider where and how writing spaces unfold in terms of the screen, we see that most use the downward vector of the scroll to extend the writing space and the infinite sidebar as a way of navigating. We gauge our place in a sliding sidebar of text, but do not necessarily have a good sense of its overall size or scope. The accumulating tail of a blog seems even less constrained, as if it were simply unrolling over time, its chunks lopped off to be archived by month or week or day. This is writing without constraint, a mode of production that has no limits in terms of quantity and frequency, and yet is very formulaic in its appearance and rhetorical structures. The graphical codes that express culturally and technically produced protocols are as intimately bound in digital environments as in analogue ones. If anything, our sensitivity to the function of graphical formats has returned from digital to print in recent experience, as acts of innovation and remediation create a dialogue across media. Our retrospective glance illuminates the bibliographical past. Suddenly it seems useful to mine it for ways of approaching the digital future, now that we have a metalanguage to describe the connection between its forms and its operations.

Books of the future, the future of books—how do we secure the place of humanity and human values at the core of a technophilic world? As we have seen, we think we know what a book is—a finite, bounded, set of sequenced pages, defined by its form as an object. We think it is a thing that we hold in our hands, finished and complete, a series of orga-

Sandra Gorman and Danny Cannizzaro, design for *Penumbra*, a multi-scaled flexible writing space (courtesy of the artists).

nized openings with recognizable and familiar physical and graphic features. But in fact, a book is a momentary slice through a complex stream of many networked conversations, versions, and fields of debate and reference across a wide variety of times and places. A book is a temporary intervention in a living field of language, images, and ideas. Each instantiation re-codifies the image of a book as an icon— whether mythic or banal, a treasure or an ordinary object of daily use.

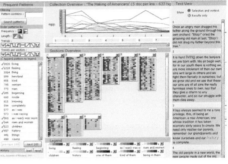

The book of the future will not simply imitate the forms of a codex migrated onto new platforms or appearing as apps on an array of devices. It will arise from an analysis of the functions of each element of design for purposes of navigation, orientation, representation, reference, and commentary and then rethink the ways the capacities of networked electronic environments can extend these functionalities and encode them in an innovative approach to design. The future book will be fluid, a conditional configuration based on a call to the vast repositories of knowledge, images, interpretation, and interactive platforms. A book will be an interface, a richly networked portal, organized along lines of inquiry in which primary source materials, secondary interpretations, witnesses and evidence, are all available, incorporated, made accessible for use.

David Small's 3D display of the Talmud (1999).

Stan Ruecker, Tanya Clement, et al., Gertrude Stein's *Making of Americans* mined for repetitive patterns and visualized (July 2008).

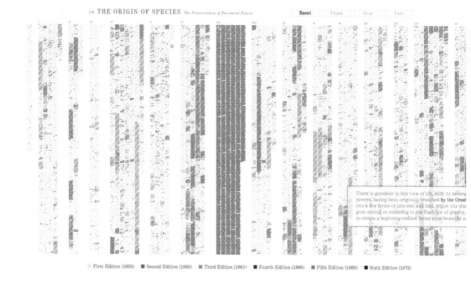

Toward humanistic design

Ben Fry, visualization of editions of Charles Darwin's *Origin of the Species* showing changes to text (2009).

We are in the incunabula period of information design. The scale of complexity challenges our conceptual models. The new condition for scholarly activity is relational and dynamic. To visualize these networked relations, communities of scholarly exchange, argument, comment, linked references, framings, and embedded citations, new conventions that do not rely on book structures are emerging. Informational derivatives of data mining, analytics, visualization, and display are increasingly a part of a reading environment in scholarly, political, and business activity. We have to imagine the design of a situation of sustained activity, a series of events. Just as Parkes makes clear that the graphical formats that became solidified in printed books had their origins in a cultural transformation that began several centuries earlier, in ways the "structuring of reasoning came to be reflected in the physical appearance of books," so the creation of digital environments for interpretative writing will refer back to earlier precedents and extend their possibilities.[248]

In essence the same critique leveled by post-structuralists against New Criticism is pertinent to the critique of formal structures—whether these are the forms and formats of information visualizations or the screen environments that reify behaviors and tasks in interface designs.[249] The "text" of the graphic expressions I have been attending to in this book is not stable and self-evident. The meaning of these expressions cannot be fixed simply by a detailed reading of their elements. The grid of wireframes is neither a set of neutral boxes for content nor a particular iconographic element. It is a structuring space whose relations create value through position, hierarchy, juxtaposition, and other features in an act of interpretation. These position us within the order of the discourse; they are *structuring regimes*. An interface is a space in which a *subject*, not a *user*, is invoked. Interface is an enunciative system. Texts and speakers are situated within pragmatic circumstances of use, ritual, exchange, and communities of practice. They are affected by it, and so is what they "read" or "receive" through an interface and they/we are produced by it. Taking critical insights from literary, cultural, and gender studies into our current practice will invigorate interface design, as will cross-cultural perspectives. Many designers, such as Dunne and Raby, Garnet Hertz, and Matt Ratto, take notions of critical interface and critical making as ways to intervene in social conditions. In their work, "critical" is closely aligned with "activist" and their designs are meant to prompt action and change. But the performance of critical thought does not necessarily have an instrumental aim. By contrast, merely reading an interface with the same techniques we used to read *Young Mr. Lincoln,* or following psychoanalytic arguments into a new realm of semiotic analysis, is a rather tedious and predictable path.[250] Though this might have some value in the undergraduate classroom, as the unpacking of ideological subtexts fascinates the young, the real challenge is in conceptualizing the spaces of interfaces that engage humanistic theory.

When we finally have humanist computer languages, interpretative interfaces, and information systems that can tolerate inconsistency among types of knowledge representation, classification, fluid ontologies, and navigation, then the humanist dialogue with digital environments will have at the very least advanced beyond complete submission to the terms set by disciplines whose fundamental beliefs are antithetical to interpretation.

The critical design of interpretative interface will push beyond the goals of "efficient" and "transparent" designs for the organization of behaviors and actions, and mobilize a critical network that exposes, calls to attention, its madeness—and by extension, the constructedness of knowledge, its interpretative dimensions. This will orchestrate, at least a bit, the shift from conceptions of interface as things and entities to that of an event-space of interpretative activity.

We must redress the odd amnesia that has come with the exigencies and tasks defined by digital media and recall our humanist commitment to interpretation. This means embracing ambiguity and uncertainty, contradictions and the lack of fixity or singularity. No file is ever self-identical, and certainly no file is ever the same twice. All expressions in human systems are constitutive, non-representational, and content models. Forms of classification, taxonomy, or information organization embody ideology. Ontologies are ideologies, through and through, as naming, ordering, and paramaterizing are interpretative acts that enact their view of knowledge, reality, and experience and give it form. All acts of migration from one medium to another, one state of instantiation to another, are mutations. The antidote to the familiarity that blinds us is the embrace of parallax, disaggregation of the illusion of singularity through comparatist and relativist approaches, and engagement with fragmentation and partial presentations of knowledge that expose the illusion of seamless wholeness. Veils of illusion are replaced with other illusions. We know this. But acknowledging the refracting effect of individual interpretations across multivalent views creates a restless engagement with the acts of knowing. More attention to acts of producing and less emphasis on product, the creation of an interface that is meant to expose and support the activity of interpretation, rather than to display finished forms, would be a good starting place.

Designing Graphic Interpretation

As a scholarly act, interpretation has almost always been textual, based on close reading, and intimately bound to the graphic form of the work to which it attaches. None of this is exclusively true any longer. To imagine new intellectual forms of interpretation is also to design the spaces and supports that structure interpretative acts. If the armature of print, now much imitated in electronic environments, has organized argument to accord with its conceptual capacities, then what will the emerging features of networked and digitally supported interpretation be like? How will they differ from those that have instructed our patterns of thought for millennia?

Innovative graphic armatures will extend our capacities to create associative arguments in digital space, creating the support for extensive interpretative activities among textual and visual artifacts. But interpretation may also take distinctly visual form. Think about a walk through a museum exhibition or a tour of a foreign city. The guide calls features of the cultural history into focus in ways that are not evident to an unfamiliar visitor. The next day in the city, or at the next exhibition, new graphical arrangements appear. The landscape changes its juxtapositions and elements, and requires a new explication. The museum rearranges walls, narratives, and frameworks of interpretation in new visual, spatial acts of interpretation. Reading graphical environments in analog or digital space and spatializing arguments through graphical means are two aspects of graphic interpretation. The first is a form of critical literacy, the second a compositional activity.

The dream of a full-fledged hypermedia that allows us to compose in a constellationary mode, with associations, links, and faceted views of an argument or narrative has been extended by the automatic protocols of analysis and processing that optimize computational capacities for synthesis and display. We integrate documents, files, data mining, visualization, mapping, and thickly linked references and citation trails on the fly. Scholars or creative writers may still have some retraining ahead to think differently about texts in electronic spaces, using their capacities to shape discourse, but as the conceptual habits shift, the technological support structures develop. Diagrammatic writing that integrates human and machine protocols of composition is emerging, and with it, the need to specify its critical properties.

How can we describe the way interpretative activity looks and acts in current electronic spaces and displays, and across a whole host of new conventions? Innovations in graphic conventions have arisen to support the scholarly activity of glossing, commentary, reference, and mediation, but also data mining, network analysis, topic modelling, and other interpretative protocols aided (or performed) by computational means. That said, only a handful of imaginative writing practices have managed to break free of the square frames and mechanical aesthetics imposed by conventions of print. One striking example is the customized designs of *Vectors* and its offshoot, *Scalar*, notable for their graphical novelty and imagination. Few of these innovations have become standard practice, at least not yet, but they point toward the possibilities of thinking graphically about interpretation and/as interface and/as argument. A wide range of media types will be mobilized for interpretation in ways that take up the mashup, remix activity of popular culture as well as realizing the scholarly aspirations that shaped the pastiche environment of Aby Warburg's Mnemosyne project.

Artists and innovative writers played with visual and spatial writing within the avant-gardes of the twentieth cen-

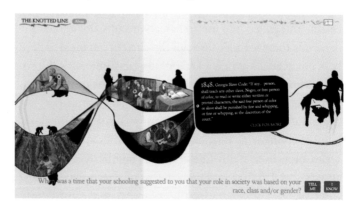

Experiments using Knotted Line in design and composition.

tury, but few if any of those radical works changed the shape of critical or scholarly conventions put into place centuries earlier. In spite of the networked condition of textual production, the design of digital platforms for daily use has hardly begun to accommodate the imaginative possibilities of constellationary composition, graphic interpretation, and diagrammatic writing. We may use mind mapping or other schematic approaches to outline a plan, sketch an argument, organize information flows, or do other tasks that abstract process into graphic forms. We may read through our links and click trails, follow our associations of thought in tracking one thing after another through browsers and faceted searching. But very few acts of composition are diagrammatic, constellationary, or associative. Fewer are visual or spatial. The predominant modes of composition in digital displays have remained quite linear, even when they have combinatoric or modular underpinnings. We know interpretation can be spatialized using architectural, topographic, or exhibition metaphors for activity in scholarly realms, poetic practice, or other activities in digital environments.

The integration of flexible spaces of writing and extensible ways of organizing relations among units of argument along with the capacities for computational analysis and processing integrated into our imaginative and scholarly work demands that we think through the current potential as surely as our predecessors worked out the conventions of the codex through practices of reading and use. The conventions and capacities of screen display and format features, the computationally enabled processes of analysis, and the flexibility of configuring relations and boundaries at different scales allow us to write differently and familiarly using digital affordances. Do they make new forms of interpretation as well? The idea of integrating the computational capabilities

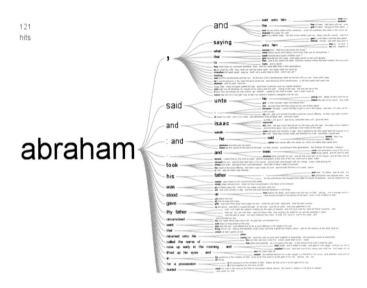

of social media, live feed, linked and hyperlinked references and resources, data mining, and so on, makes us see the relations among units and lines of argument in diagrammatic modes. When a topic map generates my understanding of a text and I cite a search query constructed through a set of different variables as a document, ephemeral though it is, then the time-scale of ephemerality factors ever more radically into the interpretative act. The search I perform with one string of characters today yields a different result tomorrow, and the first page of any search result will change constantly. The contingent character of any act of textual production increases exponentially with the expansion of data on which it draws for its composition and display. The conditional text has become the norm.

Diagrammatic composition is increasingly put at the service of scholarship, argument, or imaginative projects, and the constellationary nature of branches and links, and shifting figures of form and/as content, is increasingly familiar,

Word trees as text visualization.

even habitual. Where and when interpretative acts take place in the click trail and movement through and across different modalities of display is a pressing question when screen spaces, computational capacities, and constellationary argument and a diagrammatic approach to composition also include the synthesis of many voices, authors, and contributions with and without attribution. Our understanding of acts of interpretation shifts when data aggregation and natural language processing produce artifacts shaped by programming protocols. These are human artifacts, of course, and the algorithms are their own form of writing, but authorship as extraction, compression, reduction, and synthesis performed across works by multiple authors, centuries, and works, is a different "authorship" than that of the past. The fluid texts of Homer, the multiple authors of the Bible, the attribution issues raised by Shakespeare—these are dramatic historical examples of what is increasingly a common condition. The author whose identity was questioned and death proclaimed by post-structuralist critics in the twentieth century may become a rare anomaly. Collective authorship, the fluid migration of text circulating and changing through social media and the medium of the social network, is increasing as a phenomenon. New modes need not replace older ones in a media ecology, but the novelty by which we recognize innovation crosses quickly into familiar habit.

Topic maps, network diagrams, circular displays of text/trees, word clouds, mind maps, and other ways of distributing text in non-linear ways have come into our conceptual vocabulary. The flexibility and re-inscribability of screen space make use of accordion folding panels, drop-down menus with their stair-stepped inventory of increasingly detailed granularity, sliding panels, and other redistributions of screen real estate. Pop ups, displays that can be closed down

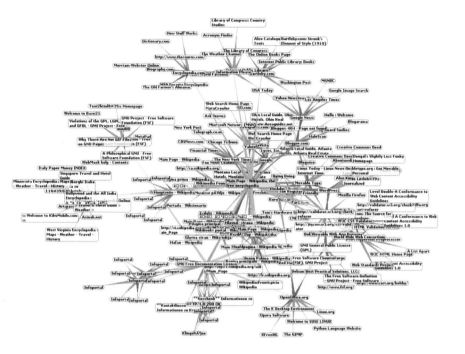

to a single bar, menus that expand in the sidebar, or toolbars/ navigation bars that appear/disappear and can be called back into play are all now part of organization or navigational features. Axes that open as the line on which an array is displayed along an orthogonal projection could be used in the same manner as the rod that organizes the cards in a card catalogue drawer. Tactile manipulation of text onscreen and the rewrite capacities of responsive media also shift conceptual practices so that we move through the illusion of virtual spaces whose dimensions are zones of argument. Elements can be laid out in illusory space, but we move through them as they reconfigure in response to our queries, our nodes of attention. What we do not attend to goes away, or persists, depending, as the extensible repository responds to our ac-

Network analysis
of Wikipedia
and the WWW.

tivity and reconfigures in a just-in-time arrangement. The flexible dimensions of screen space promote macro- and micrographia. Screen surface has no limits to its horizontal or vertical dimensions; scalable relations, topological dimension, and writing in n-dimensional space (ability to open an infinite number of spaces that are graphically displayed but semantically driven) are all features of electronic space. Digital display supports the same functions as the printed page: presentation (what appears, the "telling" in narrative parlance), representation (what it alludes to and/or the "told" borrowing again from narrative theory); computational processing (data mining, etc.); navigation (wayfinding); orientation (position within frames); reference (links); and social exchange (networked communication). These digital features mimic the functions of a book page, but add the additional functionality of re-inscribability, computational processing and analysis, real-time refresh, and networked environments.

Specific challenges arise from changes in scale of the repositories and data to which networked environments provide access. Distant reading and views of large data make it difficult to follow threaded conversations at different degrees of granularity, so all displays have to be points of entry, interfaces into content. Multiple tables of contents can be drawn from a single set of texts, database records, and metadata entries. These can be juxtaposed to semantic web diagrams mapping textual connections based on proper names, place names, frequency distributions of word combinations, or other textual features.

The combination of abstract information visualizations, mediating viewers' relation to large corpora of texts, and the ability to use such visualizations as access points to digitized documents or files makes the relation of large scale and minute granularity readily possible. The multiple views in online games offer some contributions for thinking about the ways we can navigate complex interactions among the multiple players or scholars. To display the faceted aspects of scholarship as a social and collaborative activity we will have to activate multiple dimensions of interpretation. An infinite number of interpretative lines can be extended as sightlines of inquiry, reference, contestation, debate across a discourse field (defined according to criteria determined in each instance). Navigation and argument will merge.

Interpretation in electronic space is, as we have pointed out elsewhere, n-dimensional.[251] At any point in a scholarly text an infinite number of interpretative lines can be extended as lines of inquiry, reference, contestation, debate. The implications for design are that we shift from the univocal to polyvocal text. We can borrow from the conventions of electronic games and offer multiple views simultaneously. Displays designed for navigation or reading or organized topic maps or semantic webs all complement each other without redundancy, as long as the relations among them are made explicit through shared clues such as common elements or reference frames.

Dynamic tensions between upload and download shift interpretative activity.[252] The click trails are captured, data in their own right, even as the interface obscures other aspects of its activity: its stealth relationship to networks, to the "mother ship" that monitors everything to promote related objects and suck information back from the transactions of users into the mega-cloud of networked consumer culture. The convenience of portability, flexibility, increasingly able to contain marks of reading, search trails and tags, the whole "thought mesh" of our processing trumps any paranoia or concern about mere privacy or property, especially for a younger generation living their lives in networked display of their personal lives. Their sense of self and other is without distinctions, they are made in the web of constant exchange, texts, tweets, messaging, talk, unbounded and nodal rather than autonomous and contained. So the information spaces they are comfortable inhabiting have the same quality, unbounded and rhizomatic.

How can we create fragmented and correlated points of view that connect one mode of analysis and display to another in a way that makes their connections legible? Frequent citations point to a domain of knowledge, shape it, expose the internecine workings of its conversations and exchanges. The social life of texts includes the imaginative potential of feedback loops prompting and remarking on production and composition. Familiar conventions work through acts of generative and performative engagement.

We are learning to read and think and write along rays, arrays, subdivisions, and patterns of thought. How can the flexible morphology of screen display enable framing, enframing, embedment, entanglement, hierarchy, listing, and other schematic strategies of composition? These involve the production of multi-linear discourse as well as non-linear modes (even though the alphanumeric sequence will persist, visual, audio, tactile, and simulacral modes will increase).

Embedding and entangling texts is not only easy in manuscript form, it is almost irresistible. In handwritten drafts of contemporary texts such practices continue to be the norm. Wandering lines, insertions, deletions of branched options, thoughts that begin and end, are dropped, aborted, abandoned, their unfinished lines broken partway through their expression—these are the ways our associations work in composition. Art historians laid out their slide lectures on the light table in complex arrays of argument and then had

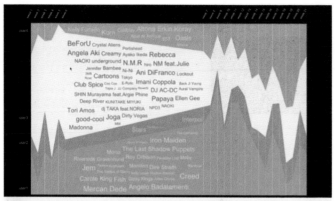

Tag River - Angus Forbes & Basak Alper
from **Angus Forbes** 1 year ago / (cc)(i)(s) [NOT YET RATED]

to compress the associative structure into side by side pairs to meet the constraints of the slide projectors. Again, Warburg's *Mnemosyne* project beckons toward the future, not just for image-based interpretations. At every point, a text suggests directions that cannot be followed in a strict linear pattern, and we prune and weed constantly because convention has required us to do so. The physical future of forms and formats, new devices and platforms, means of access, use, combination, and sequence, will merge multi-modal cross-platform and trans-device production into a discursive field. The social futures of activities and effects, concepts and practices, exist in an unbounded and often unframed and non-delimitable tissue of associated links and trails. The symbolic future of communication and community, of making public and creating shared points of reference and understanding, will create collective memory in the lived experience of the noösphere. [See Window 8, the "book" of the future]

Angus Forbes,
Tag River.

Humanists work with fragmentary evidence when researching cultural materials. They produce interpretations, not repeatable results. We have to find graphical conventions

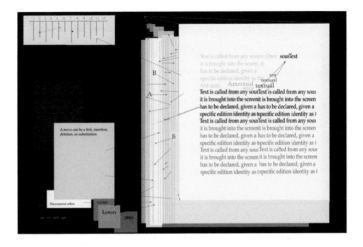

to show uncertainty and ambiguity in digital models, not just because these are conditions of knowledge production in our disciplines, but because the very model of knowledge itself that gets embodied in the process has values whose cultural authority matters very much. Multiple imaging modes that create palimpsestic or parallax views of objects make it more difficult to imagine reading as an act of recovering truth, and render the interpretative act itself more visible. The task of modeling diversity, of exposing the differences among ontologies as ideologies, has a dramatic role to play in dislodging the centrism of Western epistemologies, in particular those grounded in the administrative sensibility with its perverse attachment to control through standardization and normalization. The differential algebra of the humanistic world always has a factor of experience in it, a recognition that knowing is situated in lived lives, human beings, whose individual experience is always in process, always interpretative. Will we think differently because of the ways interpretation takes shape across networked contingencies? Or are these material conditions producing us as new subjects of a dis-

I.nterpret sketch.

tributed imagination? Are we merely part of an emerging constellation of potentialities for realization of aspects of knowledge design and interpretative acts that are closer to our once-sensible reading of natural and cultural landscapes? Perhaps we are reawakening habits of associative and spatialized knowledge we once read and through which we knew ourselves. We may yet awaken the cognitive potential of our interpretative condition of being, as constructs that express themselves in forms, contingently, only to be remade again, across the distributed condition of knowing.

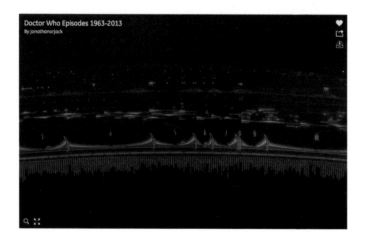

Dr. Who episodes.

Afterword

Technological advances integrating computational capacities with lived experience will soon blur the perception of analogue phenomena and digital projections in our daily lives. Embedded files triggered by environmental sensors or ambient experience provoked by our presence will situate us in a hybrid sensorium. Utopian or dystopian, this future is upon us. Navigating the complexities of its extensible frontiers, the circle of collective memory and activity whose center is everywhere and boundary constantly reconfiguring around the individually situated point of view, the processing we think of as our "own" experience will be both more complicated and more seamless.

The expansion of access to any and all stored data that can be repurposed and remediated nearly boggles the mind. Capacities may well outstrip fluencies. The ability to think in and with the tools of computational and digital environments will evolve only as quickly as our ability to articulate the metalanguages of our engagement. We have to have a way to talk about what it is we are doing, and how, and to reflect critically and imaginatively if tools of the new era are to be means to think with, rather than instruments of a vastly engineered ideological apparatus that merely has its way with us.

If this vision verges too much on fiction for some rational souls, convinced that we merely have a challenge of data curation and management on our hands, then at the very least, we can address the pragmatic need to engage new forms of argument. Where are the manuals of rhetoric for the electronic age? What grammars will take their place beside those that stood for years, such as those of the great fourth century BCE Sanskrit scholar, Panini, and the Latinist, Priscian, from the beginning of the sixth CE? What treatises in rhetoric will expand the principles of ethos, pathos, and logos from Aristotle or build on Quintilian's concepts of invention, arrangement, style, presentation, memory, and action in ways appropriate to the media of our times? Such guides would have to engage with the tenets of graphical knowledge production, with order and sequence, hierarchy and proximity, temporal dimensions and spatial axes, with concepts of derivation and replication, of continuity and juxtaposition, as ordering elements of communicative systems.

If I gesture toward a distributed environment as the plane of rhetorical action, then, I am not doing it in the spirit of science fiction and special effects, but with the understanding that embracing the design challenges for creating new forms of knowledge modeling and ways to speak about them is a task for humanists. Our responsibility is to infuse the engineering capability with an imaginative sensibility.

What kind of interface exists after the screen goes away? A hand-held device that conjures the data world into view? I touch the surface of my desk and it opens to the library of the world? My walls are display points, capable of offering the inventory of masterworks from the world's museums and collections into view? Or of displaying a virtual rendering of any space, place, built or natural, that might exist or have existed in any place or time? I write a novel that is a performance making use of avatar actors whose lives were lived before I was born but whose images activate the stage in a theater of all possibilities? Which lifecycles of thought and processing actually add engagement back into data in forms for collective access and shared memory? Who uses my thoughts later, recruiting them from their stored condition into reanimated use?

Blind narcissism and emergent collectivity collide, commingle, combine in a dazzling interplay of self-realization in representational forms and the potential of engagements with the other. Performance and dialogue, participation and production, consumption and upload contributions are all at play, along with the many filtering capacities and exigencies that map the semantics of my world view into an experiential field. Worlds to come and worlds that are with us intertwine. The ecology of the vast symbolic world has to be supported by a material infrastructure of sustainability and responsibility, and turning our back on the real is no way to guarantee the virtual. But social issues alone will not engage the political imagination or resolve the pressures of the world. People get lost in games for a reason; their affective connection is so powerful it trumps mere physical needs. The satisfactions of thinking, embodied and engaged, have their own addictive urgencies.

Theoretical premises also shift, bringing theories of media archaeology and complex adaptive systems into play. The animate and inanimate worlds, once divided absolutely by description and assumption, no longer seem to be as binaristic as they once were. The tools of complexity apply to each, and new materialisms offer ways of thinking about sentience that let us ease the border tensions of older models. The interpretative and the empirical need not exclude each other. So the graphic grammar of an emerging visual system inclined to present the embodied, situated, circumstantial, and fragmentary quality of knowledge will embrace specificities and particularities even as it makes possible the social mediation of communicative exchange. Thought forms expressed in the constellationary field may be abstracted and studied for their configuration of knowledge as well as their content, and the organizing orders of graphical expression will take on their own legibility. We won't have to translate grids, outlines, schematic patterns, and configured fields into verbal language any more than we do now, comparing two columns of quantitative data displayed in parallel bars on a chart, but we will have a greater capacity to express ourselves in those forms and formats. We will use the interpretative force of graphical rhetoric as a gesture language of intellectual life, as a way of shaping our communication using the variable dimensions of time and space in ways that print could only hint at, recording as it did the layered, palimpsestic traces of individual and collaborative activities on the enduring substrate of its material surfaces. In the endlessly rematerialized refresh that draws the rhetorical field anew in each instance, how will we know where we are, from where we speak and write, to whom and in relation to what marker and milestones that give us purchase on the cognitive frameworks of experience? The challenge opens with this view, into the studio laboratory of knowledge design, where we sit at the consoles of workstations meant to help engineer and imagine the creation and implementation of a diagrammatic and constellationary rhetoric, of writing in the infinitely extensible field populated by new conventions of legibility that structure and organize expression and communication. Then the workstation dissolves into infinite play of text and task, knowledge as performance and invention, a cognitive engine engaged with the collective life of embodied mind.

Endnotes

1 **Oliver Grau** ed., *Imagery in the 21st Century* (Cambridge, MA: MIT Press, 2011) and **Gerry Beegan**, *The Mass Image* (NY: Palgrave, 2008).

2 **Johanna Drucker**, "Reading Interface," *PMLA* (Fall 2012) and "Performative Materiality and Theoretical Approaches to the Interface," *Digital Humanities Quarterly* 7.1 (2013), http://digitalhumanities.org:8080/dhq/vol/7/1/000143/000143.html. Concepts of performativity invoked throughout are based on **John L. Austin**, *How to Do Things with Words* (Oxford: Clarendon, 1962).

3 **James Elkins**, *The Domain of Images* (Ithaca: Cornell University Press, 2001), **Barbara Stafford**, *Good Looking* (Cambridge: MIT, 1998), and **Martin Jay**, *Downcast Eyes* (Berkeley and Los Angeles: University of California Press, 1993).

4 Exceptions can always be found and remarkable work found its public face in 1960s and 1970s exhibits such as **Kynaston McShine**'s *Information* (NY: MoMA, 1970) and **Jack Burnham**'s *Software* (NY: Jewish Museum, 1970), organized by **Jasia Reichardt** in the same period.

5 Rhind papyrus, http://ontology.buffalo.edu/smith/book/austrian_philosophy/CH8.pdf; **R. Gay Robins** and **Charles C. D. Shute**, *The Rhind Mathematical Papyrus: An Ancient Egyptian Text* (London: British Museum Publications Limited, 1987); Anon., "Euclid," *Encyclopedia Britannica*, 1911, vol. 9, 880. http://encyclopedia.jrank.org/EMS_EUD/EUCLID.html.

6 **David C. Lindberg**, *Theories of Vision from Al-Kindi to Kepler* (Chicago and London: University of Chicago Press, 1976).

7 **Harry Robin**, *The Scientific Image* (NY: W.H. Freeman and Co., 1993).

8 **William Ivins**, *Prints and Visual Communication* (Cambridge, MA: Harvard University Press, 1952) and *Art and Geometry* (Cambridge, MA: Harvard University Press, 1946).

9 **Estelle Jussim**, *Visual Communication and the Graphic Arts* (London: Bowker, 1983), provides an excellent example of careful attention to the intersection of technical and aesthetic effects in print.

10 **Roland Barthes**, "The Photographic Message," *Image/Music/Text*, Stephen Heath trans. (NY: Hill and Wang, 1977), 15-31.

11 **Friedrich Kittler**, *Discourse Networks* (Palo Alto: Stanford University Press, 1992) is the starting point, but more recently, **Jussi Parikka**, **Wolfgang Ernst**, **Lisa Gitelman**, **Matthew Kirschenbaum**, and **Erkki Huhtamo** have made major contributions to this discussion.

12 **René Thom**, "Stop Chance! Stop Noise!" *SubStance* 40 (1982): 9-21.

13 **Martin Kemp**, *Visualizations: The Nature Book of Art and Science* (Berkeley: UC Press, 2000); **Eugene Ferguson**, *Engineering and the Mind's Eye* (Cambridge. MA: MIT Press, 1992); and **Bernard Cohen**, *Album of Science: From Leonardo to Lavoisier, 1450-1800* (NY: Scribners, 1980).

14 **Vitruvius**, *De Architectura*, translated as *The Ten Books on Architecture*, Morris Hickey Morgan ed., http://www.perseus.tufts.edu/hopper/text?doc=Perseus%3Atext%3A1999.02.0073&redirect=true.

15 **Sebastiano Serlio**, *Regole generali d'architettura* (1537), in Vaughan Hart and Peter Hicks eds., *Sebastiano Serlio on Architecture,Volume One: Books I-V of 'Tutte l'opere d'architettura et prospetiva'* (New Haven & London: Yale University Press, 1996).

16 Andrea Palladio, *I quattro libri dell'architettura* (1570), http://secure.octavo.com/editions/pldarc/.

17 Giambattista Della Porta, *De humana physiognomonia libri IV* (1586) and Johann Kaspar Lavater, *Physiognomische Fragmente zur Beförderung der Menschenkenntnis und Menschenliebe* (1775–1778).

18 Alphonse Bertillon, *Identification anthropométrique* (Melun: Imprimerie Administrative, 1893); but see also the Bertillon System, http://cultureandcommunication.org/deadmedia/index.php/Bertillon_System.

19 Etienne-Jules Marey, *La Méthode graphique dans les sciences expérimentales et particulièrement en physiologie et en médecine* (Paris: G. Masson, 1878). See also James J. Hodges, http://transliteracies.english.ucsb.edu/post/research-project/research-clearinghouse-individual/research-reports/the-indexical-imagination-marey%E2%80%99s-graphic-method-and-the-technological-transformation-of-writing-in-the-nineteenth-century.

20 Ann Bermingham, *Learning to Draw: Studies in the Cultural History of a Polite and Useful Art* (New Haven: Yale University Press, 2000).

21 Leonardo da Vinci, *Treatise on Painting*; see also Charles Bargue, with Jean-Léon Gerome, *Drawing Course* (Paris: ACR editions, 2003).

22 Owen Jones, *The Grammar of Ornament* (London: Day and Son, 1856).

23 David Pierre Giottino Humbert de Superville, *Essai sur les signes inconditionnels dans l'art* (Leiden: 1827).

24 Molly Nesbit, *Their Common Sense* (London: Black Dog Publishing, 2000), 23.

25 Charles Blanc, *Grammaire des Arts du dessin* (Paris: Hachette, 1880).

26 Walter Crane, *The Bases of Design* (London: Bell and Sons, 1898) and *Line and Form* (London: Bell and Sons, 1925).

27 John Ruskin, *The Stones of Venice* (London: Smith, Elder, and Co., 1851-53).

28 Johanna Drucker and Emily McVarish, *Graphic Design History: A Critical Guide* (second edition; Upper Saddle River, NJ: Pearson Prentice Hall, 2012).

29 Joseph Moxon, *Mechanick Exercises* (London: Joseph Moxon, 1694).

30 Johanna Drucker, *The Visible Word* (Chicago: University of Chicago Press, 1994); Stanley Morison, *First Principles of Typography* (NY: MacMillan Company, 1936); Frederic Goudy, *Typologia* (Berkeley and Los Angeles: University of California Press, 1940); Bruce Rogers, *Paragraphs on Printing* (NY: William E. Rudge's Sons, 1943); and Jan Tschichold, *The New Typography* (Los Angeles and Berkeley: University of California Press, 1995; Ruari McLean trans. from the 1928 German original) and *Asymmetric Typography* (NY: Reinhold Publishing, 1967; Ruari McLean trans. from the 1935 German original).

31 Tschichold, *op. cit.*

32 Paul Klee, *The Thinking Eye: Notebooks of Paul Klee* (NY: G. Wittenborn, 1964) and Wassily Kandinsky, *Concerning the Spiritual in Art* (1911).

33 Johannes Itten, *Design and Form: The Basic Course at the Bauhaus*, published 1923; and Walter Gropius, "Bauhaus Manifesto," Bauhaus Archiv, www.bauhaus.de/english/bauhaus1919/manifest1919.htm.

34 Patricia Railing, *From Science to Systems of Art: On Russian Abstract Art and Language 1910/1920 and Other Essays* (East Sussex: Artists Bookworks, 1989).

35 Wassily Kandinsky, *Point and Line to Plane* (NY: Dover, 1979; unabridged republica-

tion of the 1947 *Museum of Non-Objective Painting*; original published in 1926), 145.

36 Klee, *Thinking Eye, op. cit.*; Kandinsky, *Point and Line to Plane, op. cit.*; and **Laszlo Moholy-Nagy,** *The New Vision,* Daphne M. Hoffman trans. (NY: Brewer, Warren, and Putnam, 1932).

37 Drucker and McVarish, *Graphic Design History: A Critical Guide, op. cit.*

38 **Alain Findeli,** "Moholy-Nagy's Design Pedagogy in Chicago (1937-1946)," *Design Issues* 6.1 (Fall 1990): 5-10.

39 Laszlo Moholy-Nagy, *Vision in Motion* (Chicago: Paul Theobald, 1947).

40 **Gyorgy Kepes,** *Language of Vision* (Chicago: Paul Theobald, 1948).

41 **Edward Booth-Clibborn** and **Daniele Baroni,** *The Language of Graphics* (NY: H.N. Abrams, 1980); **Andre L'Hote,** *Les Invariants plastiques* (Paris: Hermann, 1967); **Anton Ehrenzweig, Hidden Order** *of Art* (London: Routledge and Kegan Paul, 1967).

42 **Donis A. Dondis,** *A Primer of Visual Literacy* (Cambridge, MA: MIT Press, 1973).

43 **Karl Gerstner,** *Designing Programmes* (Teufen: Arthur Nigli, 1964) and work by **Max Bill** and **Josef Müller-Brockmann.** See also **Arthur Turnbull** and **Russell N. Baird,** *Graphics of Communication* (NY: Holt, Rinehart, and Winston, 1980); **Wendell C. Crow,** *Communication Graphics* (Englewood Cliffs, NJ: Prentice Hall, 1986); and **Ken Smith** et al., *Handbook of Visual Communication Research* (Mahwah, NJ and London: Lawrence Erlbaum Associates, Publishers, 2005).

44 Gerstner, *Designing Programmes, op. cit.*

45 **Anton Stankowski,** *Visual Presentation of Invisible Processes* (NY: Hastings House, 1967).

46 **Wilhelm Worringer,** *Abstraction and*

Empathy: A Contribution to the Psychology of Style, Michael Bullock trans. (London: Routledge and Kegan Paul, 1953); first published as *Abstraktion und Einfühlung* (Neuwied: Heuser'sche Verlags-Druckerei, 1907).

47 **Carl Jung,** *Man and His Symbols* (NY: Dell, 1961).

48 **Ernst Cassirer,** *Philosophy of Symbolic Form* (New Haven: Yale University Press, 1923).

49 **Wilhelm Fuchs,** *Source Book of Gestalt Psychology* (London: Routledge and Kegan Paul, 1967) and **Ash Gabar,** *Philosophic Foundations of Genetic Psychology and Gestalt Psychology* (The Hague: Martinus Nijhoff, 1968).

50 **Christian von Ehrenfels,** "On The Qualities of Form," *Vierteljahrsschrift für wissenschaftliche Philosophie* 14 (1890): 249-292.

51 **Kurt Koffka,** "Perception: An introduction to the Gestalt-theorie," *Psychological Bulletin* 19 (1922): 531-585; but see also **Christopher Green,** "Classics in the History of Psychology," http://psychclassics.asu.edu/ Koffka/Perception/intro.htm and **W. D. Ellis,** *A Source Book of Gestalt Psychology* (NY: Harcourt Brace, 1938).

52 http://tepserver.ucsd.edu/~jlevin/gp/, http://www.queness.com/post/10347/six-gestalt-principles-in-web-design; http:// www.vanseodesign.com/web-design/ gestalt-principles-of-perception/.

53 **Rudolf Arnheim,** *Art and Visual Perception* (Berkeley and Los Angeles: University of California Press, 1954).

54 Arnheim, *ibid.,* 53.

55 **Viktor Erlich,** *Russian Formalism* (The Hague: Mouton, 1965); **Jonathan Culler,** *Structuralist Poetics* (Ithaca: Cornell University Press, 1976); and **Terry Eagleton,** *Literary Theory* (Oxford: Basil Blackwell, 1983).

56 **Roman Jakobson,** "On the Relation Between Visual and Auditory Signs," in

Selected Writings, http://www.ebooksread. com/authors-eng/roman-jakobson/ selected-writings-volume-2-oka/page-39- selected-writings-volume-2-oka.shtml.

57 **Ladislav Matejka** and **Irwin R. Titunik** eds., *The Semiotics of Art: Prague School Contributions* (Cambridge, MA: MIT Press, 1976).

58 **Nelson Goodman**, *Languages of Art* (Indianapolis and London: Hackett Publishing, 1976).

59 **Jacques Bertin**, *The Semiology of Graphics* (Madison: University of Wisconsin Press, 1983).

60 **Fernande Saint-Martin**, *Semiotics of Visual Language* (Indianapolis: Indiana University Press, 1990).

61 Saint-Martin, *ibid.*

62 **Robert Horn**, *Visual Language* (MacroVU Press, 1998) and **Connie Malamed**, *Visual Language for Designers* (Rockport Publishers, 2009).

63 This is even reflected in the title of **Phillip B. Meggs**'s classic, *Type and Image: The Language of Graphic Design* (Hoboken, NJ: Wiley, 1992).

64 **Scott McCloud**, *Understanding Comics* (NY: Harper, 1993).

65 **Erving Goffman**, *Frame Analysis: An Essay on the Organization of Experience* (London: Harper and Row, 1974).

66 **Sergei Eisenstein**, *Film Form*, Jay Leyda trans. (NY: Harcourt Brace, 1974).

67 Barthes, "The Third Meaning: Research Notes on Some Eisenstein Stills" pp. 44-68 in *Image Music Text* (NY: Hill and Wang, 1977).

68 Lindberg, *op. cit.*; **J. J. Gibson**, *The Ecological Approach to Visual Perception* (Boston: Houghton Mifflin, 1979); **R. L. Gregory**, *Eye and Brain* (Princeton, NJ: Princeton University Press, 1966); and **Stephen Kosslyn**, *Image and Mind* (Cambridge,

MA: Harvard University Press, 1980).

69 **Harold Cohen**, AARON Project, http:// en.wikipedia.org/wiki/AARON.

70 Cohen, *ibid.*

71 **Susan Kare**, http://www.computerhistory. org/atchm/macpaint-and-quickdraw- source-code/ and http://en.wikipedia.org/ wiki/MacPaint.

72 **John Maeda** and **Paola Antonelli**, *Design by Numbers* (Cambridge, MA: MIT Press, 2001); **Ben Fry** and **Casey Reas**, *Processing: A Programming Handbook* (Cambridge, MA: MIT Press, 2007).

73 **David Marr**, *Vision: A Computational Investigation into the Human Representation and Processing of Visual Information* (San Francisco: W.H. Freeman, 1982).

74 Marr, *ibid.*

75 **Janet Heine Barnett**, "Early Writings on Graph Theory: Euler Circuits and the Konigsberg Bridge Problem," http://www.eecs. berkeley.edu/~christos/classics/euler.pdf.

76 **Tableau**, "Which chart or graph is right for you," http://www.tableausoftware.com/ learn/whitepapers/which-chart-or-graph- is-right-for-you or **ManyEyes**, http://www- 958.ibm.com/software/analytics/manyeyes/ page/Visualization_Options.html.

77 **Jack H. Williamson**, "The Grid: History, Use, and Meaning," *Design Issues* 3.2 (autumn 1986): 171-86; **Howard Gray Funkhouser**, "The Historical Development of Graphical Representation of Statistical Data," *Osiris* 3 (1937): 269-404; **John E. Murdoch**, *Antiquity and the Middle Ages*, Album of Science 1 (NY: Scribner, 1984); **Barbara Tversky**, "Some Ways that Maps and Diagrams Communicate," *Spatial Cognition II - Lecture Notes in Computer Science* 1849 (2000): 72-79; **Julius T. Fraser**, *Time, The Familiar Stranger* (Amherst, MA: University of Massachusetts Press,

1987); **Fabio A. Schreiber**, "Is Time a Real Time? An Overview of Time Ontology in Informatics," pp. 283-307 in W.A. Halang and A.D. Stoyenko eds., *Real Time Computing*, Nato ASI series F.127 (1994); **M. Steedman**, "The Productions of Time," draft tutorial notes 2.0: University of Edinburgh, available at ftp://ftp.cis.upenn.edu/pub/steedman/temporality/.

78 **Franz Gnaedinger**, "Very Early Calendars," http://www.seshat.ch; **Daniel Rosenberg** and **Anthony Grafton**, *Cartographies of Time* (NY: Princeton Architectural Press, 2010); **Evelyn Edson**, *Mapping Time and Space: How Medieval Mapmakers Viewed Their World* (London: The British Library, 1997); and **Michael W. Evans**, "The Geometry of the Mind," *Architectural Association Quarterly* 12.4 (1980): 32-55.

79 Bernard Cohen, *op. cit.*; and **Roger Cook**, *Tree of Life: Images of the Cosmos* (NY: Avon Books, 1974).

80 **S.K. Heninger, Jr.** *The Cosmological Glass: Renaissance Diagrams of the Universe* (San Marino, CA: Huntington Library, 1973).

81 **Joscelyn Godwin**, *Athanasius Kircher* (London: Thames and Hudson, 1979) and *Robert Fludd* (London: Thames and Hudson, 1979).

82 **Michael Friendly**, *A Brief History of Data Visualization*, pp. 1–34 in C. Chen, W. Härdle, and A. Unwin eds., *Handbook of Computational Statistics: Data Visualization* (Heidelberg: Springer-Verlag, 2007); Funkhouser, *op. cit.*; and **Laura Tilling**, "Early Experimental Graphs," *The British Journal for the History of Science* 8.3 (Nov. 1975): 193-213.

83 Friendly, *op. cit.*, but see also Friendly's "Milestones in the History of Data Visualization," pp. 34-55 in C. Weihs and W. Gaul eds., *Classification: The Ubiquitous Challenge* (Heidelberg: Springer-Verlag, 2005).

84 These may be somewhat unfamiliar principles. For instance, the rationalization of a surface is the concept that an area or space can serve to support marks, signs, and visual features. This undertaking is unique to humans. Other animals have various sign systems and communication modes. Some make tools. But only humans create visual images and representations. Cro-Magnon culture and pictorial expression are contemporaneous, suggesting that graphical production is evidence of a particular stage of human development that involves social organization, coordination, and communication at a fairly high level of cognition. Figure/ground distinctions make use of the most fundamental logical principle: difference. While the notion that a figure and a ground are distinct is so self-evident to us as to seem unworthy of remark, this distinction underlies all human capacity for thought. **George Spencer Brown**, at the beginning of his classic work, *The Laws of Form* (London: George Allen and Unwin, 1969), states: "Make a distinction." Differentiation is the basis of knowledge production. In graphical systems, the figure/ground distinction that posits one element as a thing, an entity, and the other as its supporting ground, is not a binarism of opposites, but the articulation of a codependent system of tensions and forces. The ground is not passive, but active and generative. The third graphic principle is that the elements have to be related to a common reference that establishes their systemic character. This allows them to be read in relation to each other. Without a point of reference or a delimiting frame, the elements would just dissipate into entropy. The spatial distribution

of elements has to be constrained in relation to some common frame or ground line. They are read within a bounding and defining domain and reference. In most writing systems, the ground line serves this purpose. Even though it is usually invisible and unmarked, the ground line performs an essential function as the element that organizes meaning production. Likewise, a frame, margins, the interplay of figurative elements and ground, are all participants in a dynamic system of forces and relations. We know that the associational field is not bounded. Signs and marks are productive, suggestive, and support multiple and multi-faceted interpretation. But in practical terms, they are read within a horizon of delimitation. These principles—rationalization, difference, and framing—are fundamental to any graphical system of meaning production. The language I have used here may seem overly formal and unnecessarily theoretical, even abstruse and obscure. But perhaps this is because the theoretical principles of graphical form are so infrequently addressed. On this topic see work by **James Elkins**, **W.T.J. Mitchell**, and Nelson Goodman, the art historiography of Arnheim, and the work of thinkers in the semiotic tradition such as Barthes, Horn, and Bertin. Semiotics begins its analysis at the level of the sign; Gestalt psychology is useful for pattern recognition and visual organization. Also pertinent here are the explorations of **Louis Marin**, **Mieke Bal**, and those who took up deconstruction and worked its theoretical principles into the visual arts (among them **Jean-Claude Lejbenzstein**, **Michael Holly**, **Keith Moxey**, and **Norman Bryson**).

85 Dated to about 2100 BCE, the Umma calendar of Shulgi is the oldest extant instance of the 12 month calendar. See **Mark E. Cohen**, *The Cultic Calendars of the Ancient Near East* (Bethesda, MD: CDL Press, 1993).

86 In India, references to months and lunar and solar cyles appear in the Vedic hymns in the second millennium BCE, but calendar standards were adopted in the second and third centuries BCE from Babylonian sources. In China a lunisolar calendar was systematized around 500 BCE. In the New World, one Mayan calendar of 260 days may be as early as the sixth century BCE, though calendars based on the cycles of Venus, the moon, and other celestial bodies provided alternative methods of measuring time. The famous Aztec calendar stone was carved in the late fifteenth century and has some of the same fixed relations of spheres and quadrants as late medieval Western celestial charts. On this subject see **Emmeline Plunkett**, *Ancient Calendars and Constellations* (London: J. Murray, 1903).

87 **Robert Hannah**, *The Greek and Roman Calendars: Constructions of Time in the Classical World* (London: Duckworth, 2005).

88 The 28-day lunar cycle and its divisions are arrived at independently in other cultures, not surprisingly, as is a 360-day year.

89 **James F. Allen** and **George Ferguson**, "Actions and Events in Interval Temporal Logic," pp. 205-45 in Oliveiro Stock ed., *Spatial and Temporal Reasoning* (Boston: Kluwer, 1997). See also Allen's "Time and Time Again: The Many Ways to Represent Time," *International Journal of Intelligent Systems* 6.4 (July 1991): 341-55.

90 Drucker, "Temporal modelling," *SpecLab* (Chicago: University of Chicago Press, 2009).

91 Jennifer Burg, **Anne Boyle**, and **Sheau-Dong Lang**, "Using Constraint Logic Programming to Analyze the Chronology in *A Rose for Emily*," *Computers and the Humanities* 34 (Dec. 2000): 377-92; **P.W. Jordan**, *Determining the Temporal Ordering of Events in Discourse*, unpublished masters thesis in the Carnegie Mellon Computational Linguistics Program, 1994.

92 **Herbert Bronstein**, "Time-Schemes, Order, Chaos: Periodization and Ideology" in Julius T. Fraser, Marlene Soulsby, and Alex Argyros eds., *Time Order and Chaos* (International University Press, 1998).

93 **A.R. Millard**, "Cartography in the Ancient Near East," pp. 107-17 in J.B. Harley and David Woodward, *History of Cartography, Volume 1 - Cartography in Prehistoric, Ancient and Medieval Europe and the Mediterranean* (Chicago: University of Chicago Press, 1987).

94 **Stephanie Meece**, "A Bird's-Eye View of a Leopard's Spots. The Catalhöyük 'Map' and the Development of Cartographic Representation in Prehistory," *Anatolian Studies* 56 (2006): 1-17.

95 Millard, *op. cit.*, 113.

96 Millard, *ibid*, 109.

97 **John Rennie Short**, *Making Space* (Syracuse: Syracuse University Press, 2004), 3.

98 Short, *ibid.*, 4.

99 See Woodward, *op. cit.* for T-O maps.

100 **E. Lester Jones**, *The Evolution of the Nautical Chart* (Washington, D.C.: US Coast and Geodetic Survey, 1923), 2.

101 For more on Mercator, see Short or Woodward and Harley.

102 Short, *ibid.*, 7.

103 Jones, *op. cit.*, 3.

104 Meece, *op. cit.*, 17.

105 **Tim Ingold**, "To Journey Along a Way of Life: Maps, Wayfinding and Navigation,"

pp. 219-242 in *The Perception of the Environment* (London: Routledge, 2000).

106 **Martin Brookes**, *Extreme Measures: The Dark Visions and Bright Ideas of Francis Galton* (NY: Bloomsbury USA, 2004).

107 **Peter Dicken** and **Peter Lloyd** map, http://glynsbox.blogspot.com/2011/08/time-and-space.html.

108 **Tom Carden**, Isochronic London Underground map, http://www.wired.co.uk/news/archive/2011-03/17/isochronic-tube-map.

109 **Denise Schmandt-Besserat**, *When Writing Met Art* (Austin: University of Texas Press, 2007).

110 Diagrams, letters, hieroglyphics, Chinese characters, and other signs do represent language. See Goodman's *Languages of Art, op. cit.*, and **Geoffrey Sampson**, *Writing Systems* (London: Hutchinson, 1984) on this subject.

111 Schmandt-Besserat makes the argument that this is a developmental sequence, and that the relations between writing and drawing are determinative in the sense that advances in the organization and rules for writing help to structure visual narrative and that the latter, in turn, boosts the capacity of writing conventions.

112 Schmandt-Besserat, *op. cit.*

113 Schmandt-Besserat, *op. cit.* on grids in the third millennium BCE.

114 **Christopher Woods**, "The Earliest Mesopotamian Writing," pp. 33–50 in *Visible Language. Inventions of Writing in the Ancient Middle East and Beyond*, Oriental Institute Museum Publications 32 (Chicago: University of Chicago Press, 2010).

115 **Theodore M. Porter**, *The Rise of Statistical Thinking, 1820-1900* (Princeton: Princeton University Press, 1986).

116 **Julian Hoppitt**, "Political Arithmetic in

Eighteenth Century England," *Economic History Review* 49.3 (1996): 517.

117 Porter, *op. cit.* and also Hoppitt, *ibid.*

118 Funkhouser, *op. cit.*, 275, but see also Friendly, "Milestones," *op. cit.*

119 **Nicolas Oresme**; see also Friendly, "Milestones," *op. cit.*

120 Funkhouser, *op. cit.*, 277-8.

121 **Laura Tilling**, "Early Experimental Graphs," *British Journal for the History of Science* 8.30 (1975): 193-213. Tilling's study notes the conspicuous absence of experimental graphs in the printed texts of the eighteenth and early nineteenth centuries. She declares that although some instruments capable of creating automatic graphs, such as Wren's weather clock, were created, their records failed to excite a great deal of interest. In the 1820s, the publication of meteorological information began to be presented in graphical form, but was still so novel as to require considerable explanation. The great exception in the natural sciences was J.H. Lambert but, as she again notes, his graphs from the 1760s and 1770s were not imitated by successors. She points to the 1830s as the period of "sudden acceleration" in graphical work.

122 Funkhouser, *op. cit.*, 281.

123 See **Edward Tufte**, *The Visual Display of Quantitative Information* (Chesire, CT: Graphics Press, 1983) for the celebratory discussion of Playfair.

124 **Howard Wainer**, *Graphic Discovery* (Princeton: Princeton University Press, 2005), 11.

125 Tilling, *op. cit.*

126 **Calvin Schmid**, *Statistical Graphs* (Hoboken, NJ: John Wiley and Sons, 1983).

127 Porter, *op. cit.*

128 See Friendly http://www.datavis.ca/gallery/flo.php and Tufte, *op. cit.*

129 Friendly, *op. cit.*

130 Lorraine Daston cited by Porter, *op. cit.*, 71.

131 http://gilbrethnetwork.tripod.com/bio.html.

132 **Christiane Klapisch-Zuber**, "The Tree," pp. 293-314 in Anthony Molho, Diogo Ramada Curto, and Niki Koniordos eds., *Finding Europe: Discourses on Margins, Communities, Images ca. 13th-18th Centuries* (NY: Berghahn Books, 2007); and Cook, *op. cit.*

133 I make a distinction between the structural features of diagrams and the actions of diagrammatic interpretation, which can act in a combinatoric way on static structures.

134 **Arthur Watson**, *The Early Iconography of the Tree of Jesse* (London: Oxford University Press, 1934).

135 Klapisch-Zuber, *op. cit.*, 293.

136 **Mary Bouquet**, "Family Trees and Their Affinities: The Visual Imperative of the Genealogical Diagram," *The Journal of the Royal Anthropological Institute* 2.1 (March 1996): 43-66.

137 **Porphyry**'s commentaries on **Aristotle**'s *Commentaries* and his own *Isagogue* were translated from Greek into Latin (by **Boethius**) and Arabic, and served as key sources for Aristotelian thought in the Byzantine world. A neo-Platonist who studied with **Plotinus** and **Longinus**, Porphyry attempted a reconciliation of Platonic and Aristotelian thought, trying to preserve the idea of Platonic universals without having to put this notion into conflict with Aristotelian ideas that particulars arise first, and universals are derived from them. In the structure of his tree, the organization of categories, though it reflects a clear hierarchy, is meant to be a description of what is "a work about the expressions used to signify the sensible things around us." But the basic ontologies are presumed to exist.

138 http://plato.stanford.edu/entries/porphyry/.

139 The imprint of Porphyrian ideas is apparent in the classification system of the highly influential works of **Isidore of Seville**, considered by some to be the last great savant of the ancient world, as well as the last of the Church Fathers. Isidore's *Etymologies*, an attempt at an exhaustive compilation of human knowledge, were central to medieval learning well into the age of print.

140 **Walter Ong**, *Ramus and the Decay of Dialogue, from the Art of Discourse to the Art of Reason* (Cambridge, MA: Harvard University Press, 1958).

141 **Denis Diderot**, translation of title page in Klapisch-Zuber, *op. cit.*, 301.

142 Klapisch-Zuber, *op. cit.*, 300-1.

143 Klapisch-Zuber, *op. cit.*, 307.

144 Watson, *op. cit.*

145 Klapisch-Zuber, *op. cit.*, 295.

146 Klapisch-Zuber, *op. cit.*, 294.

147 Klapisch-Zuber, *op. cit.*, 302.

148 Klapisch-Zuber, *op. cit.*, 302.

149 Network diagrams, *Visualizing Complexity*, http://www.visualcomplexity.com/vc/.

150 **Martin Gardner**, *Logic Machines and Diagrams* (NY: McGraw-Hill, 1958).

151 **Jon Barwise** and **Gerard Allwein**, *Logical Reasoning with Graphs* (New York and Oxford: Oxford University Press, 1996), 14, but see all of chapter three.

152 Barwise and Allwein, *ibid.*, 23.

153 Barwise and Allwein, *ibid.*, 14.

154 **Jill H. Larkin** and **Herbert A. Simon**, "Why a Diagram is (Sometimes) Worth Ten Thousand Words," *Cognitive Science* 11 (1987): 65-99. The authors begin with a contrast to "sentential" representations (by which they mean sentences), but the term seems awkward.

155 Larkin and Simon, *ibid.*, 68.

156 Larkin and Simon, *ibid.*, 69.

157 **Mark D. Johnston**, *The Spiritual Logic of Ramon Llull* (Oxford: Clarendon Press, 1987).

158 Gardner, *op. cit.*, 10-11.

159 Gardner, *op. cit.*, 12.

160 Murdoch, *op. cit.*

161 A Google search will bring up many citations of Ramon Llull as computational. See **Sara L. Uckelman**, "Computing with Concepts, Computing with Numbers: Llull, Leibniz, and Boole" (2010): http://tilburguniversity.academia.edu/SaraUckelman/Papers/184828/Computing_with_Concepts_Computing_with_Numbers_Llull_Leibniz_and_Boole.

162 **Peter Apian**, *Cosmographia* (Antwerp: Christopher Plantin, 1574). For online images see: http://www.headlesschicken.ca/eng204/texts/CosmographicusLiber/index.html.

163 See the discussion of mathesis in **Daniel Crevier**, *AI: The Tumultuous History of the Search for Artificial Intelligence* (NY: Basic Books, 1993).

164 **Brian J. Ford**, *Images of Science* (London: Oxford University Press, 1993).

165 http://www.kerryr.net/pioneers/gallery/ns_leibniz6.htm.

166 **E. J. Aiton** and **E. Shimao**, "Gorai Kinzo's Study of Leibniz and the *I Ching* Hexagrams," *Annals of Science* 38 (1981): 71-92.

167 **Terence Parsons**, "The Traditional Square of Opposition," *The Stanford Encyclopedia of Philosophy* (Fall 2012 Edition), http://plato.stanford.edu/entries/square/#OriSquOpp.

168 Parsons, *ibid.*

169 **Gershom Scholem**, *Origins of the Kabbalah*, Allan Arkush trans. (Princeton: Princeton University Press, 1987).

170 Funkhouser, *op. cit.*, 369.

171 **John Venn**, *Symbolic Logic* (London: Macmillan, 1881).

172 See Gardner, *op. cit.*, Barwise and Allen, *op. cit.*, and **Sun-Joo Shin**, *The Iconic Logic of Peirce's Graphs* (Cambridge, MA and London: MIT Press, 2002).

173 Funkhouser, *op. cit.*, 369.

174 Funkhouser, *op. cit.*, 369-370.

175 **Maurice d'Ocagne**, *Traité de Nomographie. Théorie des abaques. Applications pratiques* (Paris: Gauthier-Villars, 1899).

176 Shin, *op. cit.*

177 Heine Barnett, *op. cit.*

178 http://www.gap-system.org/~history/Hist-Topics/Topology_in_mathematics.html.

179 Gardner, *op. cit.*, 55-6.

180 Shin, *op. cit.*, 16, and **J. Jay Zeman**, "Peirce's Logical Graphs," *Semiotica* 12:3 (1974): 239-56.

181 Shin, *op. cit.*, 19-20.

182 **Zeqian Shen** and **Kwan-Liu Ma**, "Path Visualization for Adjacency Matrices," *Eurographics, IEE-VGTC Symposium on Visualization* (2007), Ken Museth, Torsten Möller, and Anders Ynnerman eds.

183 For a discussion of dynamic graphics, see **Lev Manovich** and **Jeremy Douglass**, "Visualizing Change: Computer Graphics as a Research Method," in Grau, *op. cit.*, 315-38.

184 **Gary Toth** and **Don Hillger**, *Precursor: Contributors to Meteorology*, http://www.cira.colostate.edu/cira/ramm/hillger/precursor.htm.

185 **Tycho Brahe**, *De Nova Stella* (Copenhagen, 1573).

186 **John Goad**, *Astrometeorologica* (London: S. Tidmarsh, 1690).

187 **Robert Fludd**, "Meteorologica Cosmica," in Godwin, *op. cit.*

188 **Stradanus's** *Nova Reperta* (Antwerp, c1600) and **Athanasius Kircher's** large oeuvre, particularly his studies of magnetism, optics, and the subterranean world, are remarkable demonstrations of belief in the capacity of visual means to represent knowledge. Stradanus's visual approach is static, as much a saying as a showing. Though he is keen to demonstrate the inventions that have shaped the modern world, they are often presented iconically rather than dynamically. Kircher's Jesuit brethren put their considerable collective energies into his project to publish a complete presentation of his era's knowledge in a series of lavishly produced and beautifully illustrated volumes. The studies of volcanos and subterranean worlds show a keen understanding of systems and of the interrelatedness of apparently disparate phenomena. The visual language for showing change, movement, forces, and tensions remains in its infancy, however, and nothing as dramatic as the diagrams presented by Descartes in his study of weather appear amidst Kircher's pages. Like Fludd, he is still constrained by a worldview in which structures and organizations are governed by mechanistic principles. The conceptual leap from the era of Descartes/Kircher to that of Newton/Leibniz and the creation of calculus seems all the more remarkable when considered from the standpoint of innovations in graphical models.

189 **René Descartes**, *Discourse on Method, Optics, Geometry, and Meteorology*, Paul. J. Olscamp trans. (Indianapolis: Hackett Publishing Company, 2001).

190 Ford, *op. cit.*

191 Aristotle, *Meteorology*, E.W. Webster trans., http://www.classics.mit.edu; **François Arago**, *Meteorological Essays* (London: Longman, Brown, Green, and Longman, 1855); **Pierre Bertholon de Saint-Lazare**, *De l'Electricité des météores* (Lyon: Bernuset, 1787); **William Cock**, *Meteorologia*

(London: Jo. Conyers, 1670); **Louis Cotte,** *Leçons Elementaires de physique, d'hydrostatique, d'astronomie, et de météorologie* (Paris: H. Barbou, 1798); **John Dalton,** *Memoirs of the Literary and Philosophical Society of Manchester* (London: Cadell and Davies, 1798); **Leonard Digges,** *A Prognostication Everlasting* (S.I.: n. p., 1556); **H.W. Dove,** *The Law of Storms* (London: Longman, Green, Longman, Roberts, and Green, 1862); **Luke Howard,** *Barometrographica* (London: Richard and John E. Taylor, 1847); **William Lackland,** *Meteors, Aerolites, Storms, and Atmospheric Phenomena,* "from the French of Zürcher and Margollé" (NY: Scribner, Armstrong, and Co., 1874); **Elias Loomis,** *A Treatise on Meteorology* (NY: Harper and Brothers, 1868); **William Prout,** *The Bridgewater Treatises - Treatise VII: Chemistry, Meteorology, and the Power of Digestion* (London: William Pickering, 1834); **P. Francisco Resta,** *Meteorologia* (Rome: Ad Francisco Monetam, 1644); **Jérôme Richard,** *Histoire Naturelle de l'air et des météores* (Paris: Saillant and Nyon, 1770); **Thomas Robinson,** *New Observations on the Natural History of this World of Matter* (London: for John Newton, 1699); and **Joseph Taylor,** *The Complete Weather Guide* (London: John Harding, 1872).

192 **Edmond Halley,** "An Account of the Cause of the Change of the Variation of the Magnetic Needle; with a Hypothesis of the Structure of the Internal Parts of the Earth," *Philosophical Transactions of Royal Society of London* 16.179–191 (1692): 563–578.

193 On isobars, see Davy, *op. cit.,* and Prout, *op. cit.*

194 H.W. Dove, *op. cit.*

195 **Rear Admiral Fitz Roy,** *The Weather Book* (London: Longman, Green, Longman, Roberts, and Green, 1863).

196 **Francis Galton,** *Meteorographica* (London: Macmillan, 1863).

197 **Frank Waldo,** *Modern Meteorology* (NY: Charles Scribner's, 1899).

198 **Sverre Petterssen,** *Introduction to Meteorology* (NY: McGraw Hill, 1941).

199 **Edward Lorenz,** *The Essence of Chaos,* (Seattle: University of Washington Press, 1996); **Benoit Mandelbrot,** *The Fractal Geometry of Nature* (NY: Freeman, 1973); and **James Gleick,** *Chaos: Making a New Science* (London: Cardinal, 1987).

200 **Bruno Latour,** "Visualization and Cognition: Drawing Things Together," *Knowledge and Society: Studies in the Sociology of Culture Past and Present,* 6 (1986): 1-40; **Sarah Lochlann Jain,** "The Mortality Effect: Counting the Dead in the Cancer Trial," *Public Culture* 22:1: (2010): 89-117; **Ted Porter,** *Trust in Numbers: The Pursuit of Objectivity* (Princeton, NJ: Princeton University Press, 1995); **Margo Anderson,** "The Census, Audiences, and Publics," *Social Science History* 32:1 (Spring 2008): 1-18; **Margo Anderson,** "Quantitative History," pp. 246-63 in *The Sage Handbook of Social Science Methodology,* William Outwaite and Stephen Turner eds. (London: Sage Publications, 2007); **Michael Lynch** and **Steve Woolgar,** "Introduction: Sociological Orientations to Representational Practice in Science," *Human Studies* 11 (1988): 99-116; and **Karin Knorr-Cetina** and **Klaus Amann,** "Image Dissection in Natural Scientific Inquiry," *Science, Technology, and Human Values* 15 (1990): 259.

201 **Henning Griethe** and **Heidrun Schumann,** "Visualizing Uncertainty for Improved Decision Making," *SimVis* (2006): 143-156; **Josh Jones, Remco Chang, Thomas Butkiewicz,** and **William Ribarsky,** "Visualizing Uncertainty for

Geographical Information in the Terrorism Database," SPIE Defense and Security Symposium (2008), dvg.uncc.edu/publications/index.html; **Alan M. MacEachren, Anthony Robinson, Susan Hopper, Steven Gardner, Robert Murray, Mark Gahegan,** and **Elisabeth Hetzler,** "Visualizing Geospatial Information Uncertainty: What We Know and What We Need to Know," *Cartography and Geographic Information Science* 32.3 (2005): 139-160; **Ben Shneiderman** and **Alex Pang,** "Visualizing Uncertainty: Computer Science Perspective," National Academy of Sciences Workshop, March 3-4, 2005, http://www.cs.umd.edu/hcil/pubs/presentations/NAS-VisUncertainty6_files/frame.htm; **Meredith Skeels, Bongshin Lee, Greg Smith,** and **George Robertson,** "Revealing Uncertainty for Information Visualization," Microsoft Publications, http://research.microsoft.com/pubs/64267/avi2008-uncertainty.pdf; **Audrey Elizabeth Wells,** *Virtual Reconstruction of a Seventeenth-Century Portuguese Nau,* 2008, Master's Thesis, Texas A&M University, Visualization Sciences, repository.tamu.edu/bitstream/handle/1969.1/86071/Wells.pdf.

202 Johanna Drucker, "Humanities Approaches to Graphical Display," *Digital Humanities Quarterly* 5.1 (2011); http://www.digitalhumanities.org/dhq/vol/5/1/000091/000091.html.

203 Drucker, "Performative Materiality," *op. cit.*

204 A paraphrase of Edward Tufte's title; see Tufte, *op. cit.*

205 **Martin Campbell-Kelly** and **William Aspray,** *Computer: A History of the Information Machine* (Boulder: Westview Press, 2004).

206 The classic text on distributed cognition is **Edwin Hutchins,** *Cognition in the Wild* (Cambridge, MA: MIT Press, 1995).

207 See **Ray Kurzweil,** *The Age of Spiritual Machines* (NY: Penguin, 2000) for an introduction to **Morton Helig, Myron Krueger,** and **Jaron Lanier.**

208 **Douglas Engelbart,** 1968 mouse demo, sloan.stanford.edu/mousesite/1968Demo.html; and **Ivan Sutherland,** 1963 Ph.D. Thesis from Massachusetts Institute of Technology, republished by the University of Cambridge as "Sketchpad, A Man-Machine Graphical Communication System," *Technical Report* 574 (2003).

209 On Alan Kay, see Campbell-Kelly and Aspray, *op. cit.*; on Xerox Parc see Malcolm Gladwell, "Creation Myth: XEROX Parc, Apple, and the Truth About Innovation," *The New Yorker* (May 16, 2011); **Michael A. Hiltzik,** *Dealers of Lightning: Xerox PARC and the Dawn of the Computer Age* (NY: HarperCollins, 1999); **Jerome Bruner,** *Actual Minds, Possible Worlds* (Cambridge, MA: Harvard University Press, 1987); **Jean Piaget,** *The Child's Construction of Reality* (London: Routledge and Kegan Paul, 1955.)

210 See for example the front page for the **Epicenter** design firm (http://www.epicenterconsulting.com/images/interface_design.jpg), though a Google search on HCI, interface design, or user-centered design will turn up a wide array of similarly worded sites.

211 Shneiderman, "Eight Golden Rules of Interface Design," http://faculty.washington.edu/jtenenbg/courses/360/f04/sessions/schneidermanGoldenRules.html faculty.

212 **Matthew Fuller,** *Behind the Blip* (Brooklyn, NY: Autonomedia, 2003).

213 **Jesse James Garrett,** "The Elements of Visual User Interface" (March 30, 2000), http://www.jjg.net/elements/pdf/elements.pdf (accessed Oct. 15, 2010).

214 **Aaron Marcus** and **Geert Hofstede**, "Cultural Dimensions and Global Web UI Design," Aaron Marcus and Associates, white paper, http://www.amanda.com/cms/uploads/media/AMA_CulturalDimensionsGlobalWebDesign.pdf (accessed Dec. 12, 2013).

215 Ben Shneiderman and **Catherine Plaisant**, *Designing the User Interface: Strategies for Effective Human-Computer Interaction* (Boston: Pearson/Addison Wesley, 2005).

216 **Mauro Manelli**, "The Theory Behind Visual Interface Design" (Nov. 20, 2002), *Developer.com*, http://www.developer.com/design/article.php/1545991/The-Theory-Behind-User-Interface-Design-Part-One.htm.

217 **Norman Long**, "UNESCO Background Paper on Interface Analysis" (Oct. 1999), http://lanic.utexas.edu/project/etext/llilas/claspo/workingpapers/multipleoptic.pdf.

218 **Brenda Laurel**, *The Art of Human-Computer Interface Design* (Reading, MA: Addison-Wesley, 1990); here I am paraphrasing Fuller, *op. cit.*, 103. See **Kaja Silverman**, *The Subject of Semiotics* (Oxford: Oxford University Press, 1983); **Paul Smith**, *Discerning the Subject* (Minneapolis: University of Minnesota Press, 1988); **Margaret Morse**, "The Poetics of Interactivity," pp. 16-33 in Judy Malloy ed., *Women, Art, and Technology* (Cambridge, MA and London: MIT Press, 2003); and other related work by Morse on television experience and flow.

219 **Jakob Nielsen**, Nielson Norman Group, http://www.nngroup.com/articles/.

220 **Steve Krug**, *Don't Make Me Think!* (Berkeley: New Riders, 2005).

221 **Erwin Panofsky**, *Perspective as Symbolic Form*, Christopher Wood trans. (Cambridge, MA and London: MIT Press, 1996) and **Victor Burgin**, "Geometry and Abjection," *AA Files - Annals of the Architectural Association School of Architecture* 15 (Summer 1987).

222 **Donald Hoffman**, "The Interface Theory of Perception: Natural Selection Drives True Perception to Swift Extinction," pp. 148-65 in Sven Dickinson, Michael Tarr, Ales Leonardis, and Bernt Schiele eds., *Object Categorization: Computer and Human Vision Perspectives* (Cambridge: Cambridge University Press, 1989); http://www.cogsci.uci.edu/~ddhoff/interface.pdf.

223 **Michel Foucault**, *The Order of Things* (NY: Pantheon, 1970).

224 **Mads Soegaard**, "Gestalt Principles of Form Perception," http://www.interaction-design.org/encyclopedia/gestalt_principles_of_form_perception.html.

225 **Gretchen Bender**, *Culture on the Brink* (NY: New Press, 1998) and Margaret Morse, *Virtualities* (Bloomington: Indiana University Press, 1998).

226 **Roy Ascott**, *The Telematic Embrace*, Edward Shanken ed. (Berkeley: University of California Press, 1998) and www.jodi.org.

227 Lev Manovich, *The Language of New Media* (Cambridge, MA: MIT Press, 2001) argues for film as a model.

228 **Humberto Maturana** and **Francisco Varela**, *The Tree of Knowledge* (Boston: Shambala, 1987) and Hoffman, *op. cit.*

229 Goffman, *op. cit.*

230 **Arianna Ciula**, "The New Edition of the Letters of Vincent Van Gogh," *Digital Humanities Quarterly* 4.2 (2010), http://digitalhumanities.org:8080/dhq/vol/4/2/000088/000088.html. See also the Van Gogh Letters Project at http://www.vangoghletters.org/vg/.

231 **Austrian Academy Corpus**, *Die Fackel*, http://corpus1.aac.ac.at/fackel/.

232 **Greg Crane**, editor in chief, Perseus Digital Library, http://www.perseus.tufts.edu/hopper/; **Encyclopedia of Chicago**, http://www.encyclopedia.chicagohistory.org/.

233 **Jonathan Harris** and **Sep Kamvar**, *We Feel Fine*, http://www.wefeelfine.org/.

234 **Roger Chartier**, "Languages, Books, and Reading from the Printed Word to the Digital Text," *Critical Inquiry* 31.1 (2004): 133–52.

235 **Anthony Grafton** and **Megan Hale Williams**, *Christianity and the Transformation of the Book: Origen, Eusebius, and the Library of Caesarea* (Cambridge, MA: Harvard University Press, 2006).

236 Grafton and Williams, *ibid.*

237 **Malcolm B. Parkes**, "The Influence of *Ordinatio* and *Compilatio* on the Development of the Book," pp. 121-142 in Parkes, *Scribes, Scripts, and Readers* (London: Hambledon Press, 1991).

238 Parkes, *ibid*, 66.

239 **Marvin J. Heller**, *Printing the Talmud* (Brooklyn, NY: Im Hasefer, 1992).

240 **Joseph R. Hacker** and **Adam Shear**, *The Hebrew Book in Early Modern Italy* (Philadelphia: University of Pennsylvania Press, 2011).

241 Heller, *op. cit.,* and Hacker and Shear, *ibid.*

242 Heller, *op. cit.,* and Hacker and Shear, *op. cit.*

243 **Jay David Bolter**, *Writing Space: Computers, Hypertext, and the Remediation of Print* (Mahwah, NJ: Lawrence Erlbaum Associates, 2000); **Michael Heim**, *Electric Language: A Philosophical Study of Word Processing* (New Haven: Yale University Press, 1987); and **George Landow**, *Hypertext 3.0: Critical Theory and New Media in an Era of Globalization* (Baltimore: Johns Hopkins University Press, 2006).

244 **Vannevar Bush**, "As We May Think," *Atlantic Monthly* (July 1945); online at http://www.theatlantic.com/doc/194507/bush; **Theodor H. Nelson**, "A File Structure for the Complex, the Changing, and the Indeterminate," *Proceedings of the ACM 20th National Conference* (1965): 84-100; **Julio Cortazar**, *Hopscotch* (NY: Pantheon, 1966); and **Joan Hall Racter** and **William Chamberlain**, *The Policeman's Beard is Half-Constructed* (NY: Warner Software Books, 1984).

245 Dada poems by Tristan Tzara, "Bulletin," and "Bilan," in *Dada*; online at http://www.dadart.com/dadaism/dada/037-Tzara.html.

246 Bolter, *op.cit.*, Heim, *op.cit.*, and Landow, *op.cit.* Jay David Bolter, (2001).

247 **Jorge Luis Borges**, "The Garden of Forking Paths," *Ficciones* (NY: Grove Press, 1968).

248 Walter Ong takes up the theme of this relation of graphical structure and intellectual systems in his study of **Petrus Ramus**, the sixteenth century humanist and pedagogue intent on reforming the teaching of Aristotelian logic and rhetoric by creating clear diagrammatic structures for its study. In describing the mental attitude that shaped the method of the late medieval logician, Ong calls attention to his use of diagrams as the basis of a radical new approach to the art of discourse central to medieval education. The sixteenth century humanist considered diagrams analogies to thought. If their organization was clearly structured, they would be capable of generating well-wrought rhetorical arguments. Ramus's method permeated the training of scholars and churchmen for generations to follow, even as the term "method" was broadly employed to describe systematic approaches to knowledge in a diversity of disciplines.

249 **Mark C. Taylor**, *Deconstruction in Context* (Chicago: University of Chicago Press, 1986); Barthes, "The Third Meaning," *op. cit.*

250 The editors, "John Ford's *Young Mr. Lin-*

coln," *Cahiers du Cinéma* (Aug. 1970); published in English trans. in *Screen* (13.3 (Fall 1972): 5-44.

251 **Jerome McGann**, "Texts in n-Dimensions: Interpretation in a New Key," *Text Technology* 12:2 (2003): 1-18, as well as my own work on I.ntepret texts. See also **Susan Hockey**, *Electronic Texts in the Humanities* (Oxford: Oxford University Press, 2000); McGann, *Radiant Textuality* (New York: Palgrave, 2001); and Drucker, "The Virtual Codex from Page Space to E-Space" (2003), www.philobiblon.com/drucker/.

252 **Peter Lunenfeld**, *The Secret War Between Uploading and Downloading* (Cambridge, MA and London: MIT Press, 2011).

Image sources

2   http://wmuphoto.wordpress.com/
category/web-art/

4   http://www.visualcomplexity.com/vc/

5   http://atlanticsmart.com/savant/
technology_truimage_
gesturetouch.html

6   http://www.axismaps.com/
blog/2009/04/virtual-globes-
are-a-seriously-bad-idea-
for-thematic-mapping/

7   http://www.ust.ucla.edu/ustweb/
Projects/columbian_expo.htm

8   http://www.united-academics.org/
magazine/earth-environment/data-
visualization-great-tree-of-life/

9   http://laelaps.wordpress.com/2007/
09/13/the-branching-bush-of-
horse-evolution/
http://s280.photobucket.com/user/
geosteve/media/nature09113-
f32.jpg.html
http://www.universetoday.com/
58521/cloud-chamber/

10 http://uciinfovisspring2011.
blogspot.com/2011/06/facebook-
interactions.html

11 http://www.medienkunstnetz.de/
assets/img/data/2999/full.jpg

23 http://similardiversity.net/gfx/
sd800.jpg

24 http://www.palladiancenter.org/
patternbooks.html

25 http://en.wikipedia.org/wiki/
Classical_order

26 http://darwinonline.org.uk/
converted/published/1845_
Beagle_F14/1845_Beagle_F14
_fig07.jpg

26 http://swiki.hfbk-hamburg.de/
Netzkunstaffairen/93

27 http://anomalus.com/public/arch2226a
/content/lectures/01/images/
pv_thompson_1.jpg

28 http://thetextileblog.blogspot.com/
2010/05/owen-jones-and-
chinese-ornament.html

30 http://www.dezenovevinte.net/
obras/av_rc_baile_files/
superville_c.jpg

31 http://www.archive.org/stream/
grammairedesarts00
blanuoft#page/649/mode/thumb

41 http://www.stankowski06.de/basis/
englishhtml/kategorien/
funktionsgrafik/funktionsgrafik.html

45 http://www.otago.ac.nz/library/
exhibitions/linnaeus/walls/

46 http://www.kovcomp.co.uk/
wordstat/wordbroc.html

48 http://radicalart.info/AlgorithmicArt/
algebra/AARON/index.html

50 http://reas.com/

51 http://cns-alumni.bu.edu/~slehar/
webstuff/orivar/orivar3.html

54 http://www.math.dartmouth.edu/
~euler/docs/originals/E053.pdf
http://mathworld.wolfram.com/
KoenigsbergBridgeProblem.html

55 http://cabinetmagazine.org/issues/
22/wertheim2.php
http://blog.host.co.in/network-
topology

61 http://www-958.ibm.com/software/
data/cognos/manyeyes/visualizations
http://www.visual-literacy.org/
periodic_table/periodic_table.pdf

62 http://www.jjg.net/elements/
pdf/elements.pdf

66 https://commons.wikimedia.org/
wiki/File:Dunhuang_star_map.jpg

http://www.w3.org/TR/xhtml-rdfa-primer/

67 http://faculty.uoit.ca/collins/research/docuburst/index.html

68 http://integral-options.blogspot.com/2012/06/what-im-reading-part-one-complex.html

70 http://euclid.psych.yorku.ca/SCS/Gallery/timelines.html

73 http://penelope.uchicago.edu/~grout/encyclopaedia_romana/calendar/antiates.html

74 http://web.mit.edu/larsb/Public/16.412/pset%204/allen94actions.pdf

77 http://commons.wikimedia.org/wiki/File:Turin_Papyrus_map_part.jpg

78 http://www.schoyencollection.com/smallercollect2.html

79 http://en.wikipedia.org/wiki/Ptolemy

80 http://commons.wikimedia.org/wiki/File:T_and_O_map_Guntherus_Ziner_1472_bw.jpg
http://en.wikipedia.org/wiki/File:Mediterranean_chart_fourteenth_century2.jpg

81 http://en.wikipedia.org/wiki/File:Mercator_1569.png

82 http://sustainablecitiescollective.com/urbantick/22004/mapping-distance-time-paris-crunch

83 http://www.tom-carden.co.uk/p5/tube_map_travel_times/applet/

86 http://primitivephysick.blogspot.com/2012/11/bills-of-mortality-and-searchers.html

88 http://commons.wikimedia.org/wiki/File:Planetary_Movements.gif

89 http://commons.wikimedia.org/wiki/File:Oresmes_diagrams.gif

90 http://en.wikipedia.org/wiki/

William_Playfair

93 http://www.museumoflondon.org.uk/Collections-Research/Research/Your-Research/RWWC/objects/record.htm?type=object&id=719785

95 http://commons.wikimedia.org/wiki/File:Arbor-scientiae.png

96 http://www.american-buddha.com/pythagsource.16.gif

97 http://commons.wikimedia.org/wiki/File:Arbor_porphyrii_(from_Purchotius%27_Institutiones_philosophicae_I,_1730).png

99 http://en.wikipedia.org/wiki/File:Tree_of_life_by_Haeckel.jpg

101 http://www.nltaylor.net/medievalia/jesse/TreeofJesseweb/Herradfish-tb.html

102 http://commons.wikimedia.org/wiki/File:Ramon_Llull_-_Ars_Magna_Tree_and_Fig_1.png

103 http://en.wikipedia.org/wiki/File:Johannesmagistris-square.jpg

104 http://commons.wikimedia.org/wiki/File:Ramon_Llull_-_Ars_Magna_Tree_and_Fig_1.png

105 http://home.comcast.net/~cerny/pub/eos03/jim-table/jim-table.html

112 http://www.burningdoor.com/dick/images/venn%20diagram.gif

114 http://www.math-cs.gordon.edu/courses/cs320/ATM_Example/SessionStateDiagram.html

115 http://en.wikipedia.org/wiki/Existential_graph

118 http://wellcomeimages.org/indexplus/obf_images/d9/00/f09f8866808c77453b3fc6003f4d.jpg

120 http://www.mhs.ox.ac.uk/wp-content/uploads/atmospherescienceatsea1.jpg

123 http://eoimages.gsfc.nasa.gov/images/imagerecords/4000/4505/